Love in the Face of Life

Jeffrey A. Klick

Dedications

To my wonderful Savior, and to my life-long companion and friend Leslie, both who have shown me, true love. And, to my family that always makes me laugh and smile and gives me strength to carry on– Andrea, Sarah, David, Brian, Jeffrey, Nicky, Lydia, Katelyn, Mackenzie, Daniel, Nathan, Havilah, Addie, Gabe, Jared, Levi, Alexis, Treya, and Neda. What a joy you all are!

Special Thanks To...

Joshua Monnington for your insightful comments and relentless pursuit of proper tenses, verb matching, and commas. And to the wonderful group of believers that call Hope Family Fellowship home. You all are a delight!

Contents

Introduction 1

1. God Started It 7

2. Love on Loan................................. 15

3. God Forced Love 27

4. Family is the Seedbed for Love 37

5. Church is a Place to Learn Love 51

6. "But I Am Right"................................ 61

7. Loving Those that Hurt You 73

8. Loving the Unlovely......................... 83

9. Saying No and Walking Away Can Be Love .. 93

10. Love Will Change the World 103

Love Lifted Me 113

Love Gems..................................... 123

About the Author 138

As you wish & death cannot stop true love; all it can do is delay it for a while · **Westley** · **The Princess Bride**

Where there is love there is life · **Mahatma Gandhi**

Tis better to have loved and lost, then never to have loved at all · **Alfred Tennyson**

Love means never having to say you are sorry
Love Story

All you need is love · **Beatles**

At the touch of love, everyone becomes a poet · **Plato**

One word frees us of all the weight and pain of life: That word is love · **Sophocles**

I have decided to stick to love; hate is too great a burden to bear · **Martin Luther King, Jr.**

I just called to say I love you · **Stevie Wonder**

God is Love · **John the Beloved**

A new commandment I give to you, that you love one another: just as I have loved you, you also are to love one another. **John 13:34**

This is *my commandment*, that you love one another as I have loved you. **John 15:12**

These things *I command you* so that you will love one another. **John 15:17**

For this is the message that you have heard from the beginning, *that we should* love one another. **1 John 3:11**

And this is *his commandment*, that we believe in the name of his Son Jesus Christ and love one another, just as *he has commanded* us. **1 John 3:23**

And now I ask you, dear lady—not as though I were writing you a *new commandment*, but the one we have *had from the beginning*—that we love one another. **2 John 1:5**

Italics added to make a point...

Introduction

By this, all people will know that you are my disciples if you have love for one another. John 13:35

The truck was rumbling down the street driven by a man who always knew where he was going. The sun was shining and the day was calm. The air was clear and the windows were down. Life was as it should be. Days like this are meant to be enjoyed.

Out of the corner of his eye, the driver saw a flash of color but an instant too late. It was no contest between boy and machine. The nine-year-old blonde boy was tossed in the air like a ragdoll after being struck landing far ahead of where the pickup truck came to a screeching halt. The boy was dead and the driver was in shock weeping, begging for this reality to be only a dream. It was instead a nightmare just beginning.

1

The father of the little boy rushed out upon hearing the horrible sounds and after one look at his son knew he was already on his way to Jesus. The driver needed help now; his son was beyond aid in this life. Running to the driver the father offered comfort, prayers, and assurances that all would be well.

The parents of the boy reached out to the driver often over the next few days and insisted that he attend the memorial service to honor the short life of their son. Reluctantly, the driver agreed.

What the driver saw and heard was beyond anything he could have imagined. Over a thousand friends gathered to celebrate a young life and support the family. People were singing, smiling, and rejoicing. Yes, there were tears and anger over the loss, but most were mixed with hope and peace beyond human understanding. Real people struggling with sorrow, pain, and heartache like everyone else, but these gatherers had something different. This multitude of people could mix tears, joy, singing, crying, pain, sorrow and peace together, and this is not normal in our world.

The man who killed the child was embraced, clearly forgiven and loved with a love that is otherworldly. How can this be? Where does this type of love come from? How does one get it? How does the strength to stand when you should be falling enter a person? The man needed to know, and he gave his life to Jesus hoping to find the answers.

The Beatles sang "all you need is love" and then proceeded to break up. "Make love not war" was one of the cries of a previous generation, yet war is a common part of millions of people's daily lives. Divorce is rampant, murder, hate, and terror fill our screens, and love does not seem to have much room in our modern life.

Many seek love but what they really are after is pleasure, sexual expression or acceptance from someone, anyone. Love has been covered in TV shows, books, movies, songs, and if one does a Google search, billions of sites will instantly pop up. Love is everywhere, or is it?

Since love has been covered from so many different perspectives, why would we need another book? In some ways that is like asking, since there is so much air, why do we need more? Or, do we really need another Hallmark Mystery movie or new Star Trek/Wars series?

Every generation needs to be reminded of love. Every person, regardless of age, needs to think about love. Love is what makes the world go around, or at least should. We all need reminding because we tend to forget when life closes in.

What marriage, couple, family, or church does not need a reminder of love? Those around us certainly need to see true love.

Here is another reason. Why is the corporate Church not known for love? The verse under the title of this chapter reveals that love is the primary identification of the disciples of Jesus. Yet, is the Church known for love or something far less?

Until everyone is walking in love, then books, movies, and every other form of communication must continue. We have not achieved love; not in our homes, churches, communities or world. There is a need. A big hole needs to be filled.

Perhaps another reason for yet another book is that no two authors are the same. We all tend to look at issues from differing viewpoints. I intend to share some truth gleaned from this life that you may not have considered.

Questions need to be answered and this book will attempt to do so. For example:

- Where does love originate?
- Why is the Bible written the way it is?
- Why can't we all just get along?
- Why did God pick the family as His model to reveal Himself to His creation?
- Why is the Church such a mess and how can we fix it?
- What should we do with all those strong opinions we may have, and how do we live with others that possess differing ones?
- How do we respond to hurts, hate, and anger?
- Is there ever a time to walk away from relationships out of true love?

There will be other questions answered along the way, but certainly, these are important or should be.

This is a book based upon a Christian worldview and the Bible will be the primary source for the answers we seek. If you are not already a believer in Jesus, I pray you will become one as you begin to understand where Love comes from, and why He came.

Love means many different things to just about everyone, but love is the universal language of heaven. Love is God's native tongue and if we hope to understand it, we must begin with the One that created it. The One that embodies it. The Author of Love.

Each chapter will include a different version of the most famous definition of love there is. Many of us have the plaque in our homes decorating our walls, but how many of us actually stop and really think about the words? How many of us really put those words into daily action in our lives?

When was the last time we read 1 Corinthians 13 and honestly considered our behavior in light of it? Are we willing to look squarely at God's definition of love and compare our thoughts, words, and actions against it?

Will we consider the consequences of implementing the truth of God's Word on this topic in our homes, churches, and nations? I pray we would.

I will make the argument that we must if we want to obey God. If we refuse, we are in disobedience to God's clearly revealed will and Holy Word. If we choose to allow the Holy Spirit to convict us and if we will actually repent and change our mind and behavior, we can change the world.

As you encounter each translation of 1 Corinthians 13:1-8 (a) please allow the Holy Spirit to renew your mind. Each group of translators carefully chose the words from the original Greek text and they all present a slightly different flavor.

God will change us as we yield to Him and His Word. Prayerfully read the following and ask the Lord to reveal a truth to you that you can implement quickly. I know He will!

1 Corinthians 13:1-8 (a) (ESV)

If I speak in the tongues of men and of angels but have not love, I am a noisy gong or a clanging cymbal.

And if I have prophetic powers, and understand all mysteries and all knowledge, and if I have all faith, so as to remove mountains, but have not love, I am nothing.

If I give away all I have, and if I deliver up my body to be burned, but have not love, I gain nothing.

Love is patient and kind; love does not envy or boast; it is not arrogant or rude.

It does not insist on its own way; it is not irritable or resentful; it does not rejoice at wrongdoing but rejoices with the truth.

Love bears all things, believes all things, hopes all things, endures all things.

Love never ends.

~~~~~~

The love of Christ stands out in all the "history of the love" as the divinest, the holiest, the strongest of all love-unequaled, unparalleled, unsurpassed - There is no love like Christ's love! Octavius Winslow (1808-1878)

1. God Started It

"I Love You."- God

In the beginning, God...before anything else was, God is. God, being self-contained, needing nothing from anyone or anything, decided to create. God certainly did not have to, and He most certainly could have done so differently.

The world we live in could have been made in any fashion the Creator desired. God could have designed His creation any way He wished. We did not have to be humans or breathe air. We could have been created to respond perfectly instead of being given a choice. We could have, but we were not.

God, for reasons only known within Himself, decided to create humans and to reveal Himself as Love.

God chose the term "Father" and God decided that the family model would be His preferred method of displaying love from one generation to another.

This is true in some of the animal kingdom, and also true in some of the human one. There are some animals that ignore their young, and this is also true in the human world. These, however, are the exception, not the rule. In our day, child abuse and neglect are still crimes. May this never change.

This natural tendency towards love is a God-given remnant from a perfect Creation. We were made in His image, and He is love. In most places, parents that abuse, neglect or kill their children are thrown into prison. Why is this, if we are simply a highly-developed animal as the evolutionist declare? Have you ever watched a nature channel? Some animals eat their young.

What we consider normal is love, not hate. Hate repels us. Love attracts us. We need love, want love, and feel a loss when we either lose it or are deprived of it. There is an emotional need for love in every one of us.

That need can only be fulfilled by the One that created it. When God created humans, He made them male and female. While many in our day are struggling with gender issues, God was not. Adam and Eve were created, hand-fashioned by the Creator in love.

We know from the early pages of Genesis that God breathed life into a pile of dust, and as this life flowed through that empty shell of a man, love was born in him.

We also know that God presented to Adam all the animals to name, and it showed him that a suitable helper was not among them. I for one am glad of this fact.

After Adam figured it out, God had this man fall asleep and performed the first surgery. A rib was taken and Eve was formed. Adam took one look at her and said, "Whoa man," or perhaps it was "woman." Both work and Adam realized that Eve was a much better mate than the animals and bugs he just had named.

Since the next verse after the above discusses the intimate relationship between man and woman, we can assume that physical and emotional love were involved.

There are many other issues to be considered, and people much wiser than I argue about these unsolvable details, but the truth is we simply do not know more than what is written. For example:

- How long were Adam and Eve in the Garden?
- How often did they resist the temptation to eat the fruit before they fell into sin?
- Was the serpent the only animal that could talk?
- Did Adam and Eve have belly buttons?
- How old were they when they sinned?
- What nationality did they resemble?
- Where are the Garden and the trees mentioned today?

None of these are earth shaking issues, but I look forward to finding out the answers someday. I also want to know what the fruit looked like, and if we will be able to eat of that tree after we die. Those answers will have to wait.

No matter your view on origins, and there are many, we all started somewhere. More important to me is that fact that we are all somewhere now, which brings me to the point of this chapter – do you know God? Do you really know the author, creator, founder of Love? Do you know Love Himself? Have you met Him personally?

God Is Love

God has chosen to reveal Himself, and the revelation is clear – God is love. Compared to the pagan gods of the past or the false ones of today, our God is amazing in His self-revelation. Consider just a sampling of verses from His Holy Word:

> O Lord, God of Israel, there is no God like you, in heaven above or on earth beneath, keeping covenant and showing steadfast love to your servants who walk before you with all their heart... 1 Kings 8:23

> The Lord your God is in your midst, a mighty one who will save; he will rejoice over you with gladness; he will quiet you by his love; he will exult over you with loud singing. Zephaniah 3:17

> See what kind of love the Father has given to us, that we should be called children of God; and so we are. The reason why the world does not know us is that it did not know him. 1 John 3:1

> Beloved, let us love one another, for love is from God, and whoever loves has been born of God and knows God. Anyone who does not love does not know God, because God is love. 1 John 4:7-8

God is love and He loves you and me. Saying that God is love is very different than saying God has love. The example I use is easy to understand. Saying God is love instead of saying God has love is like saying Jeff *is* a glass of water versus Jeff *has* a glass of water. See the difference?

If God is love then He always will act in love. I am not a glass of water. If I have a glass of water I can drain it, drink it, spill it, or break it. I can even lose it. If I am a glass of water then I will always be a glass of water and will always act like water. I can't help it.

God is love. God cannot lose it, spill it, forget it, or ignore it. He is love.

We all know this verse:

> For God so loved the world, that he gave his only Son, that whoever believes in him should not perish but have eternal life. John 3:16

For whatever reasons God may have possessed within Himself, He loved us. He still does. God loved us so much He sent His Son to die for us, so we could live. We must begin to embrace this understanding and truth. John desired for his readers to understand this truth. Consider this verse for a moment:

> So we have come to know and to believe the love that God has for us. God is love, and whoever abides in love abides in God, and God abides in him. 1 John 4:16

"Come to know" refers to a process. We gradually learn to accept the truth that in spite of who we are, what we have done, and how messed up we may be, God loves us. God does not reject us, cast us out, or despise us; He loves us.

God loves us but it doesn't stop there, for if it did, this life would be easy. God also provides others for us to share this life with, and therein lies the problem! Love requires an object, and God determined that we would all have people in our lives to learn how to love like God loves.

Jesus demonstrated perfect love as an example for us to follow:

> Greater love has no man than to lay down his life for another – John 15:13.

If we are going to learn how to love as God loved us, we will learn how to lay down our lives one for another.

Jesus showed us how and the Holy Spirit was given to empower us to make the choice of laying down our lives for others. As we continue on we will see many practical ways to walk in love, but before we move into the next chapter and begin to consider what to do with this love we have received, let's pause a moment and ponder some of the following questions.

For Our Consideration:

1. Why did God create man and woman?

2. What does it mean to you that God loves you?

3. Why do you think God chose the family model to reveal Himself to His creation?

4. What does it mean to you when John states that "God is love?"

1 Corinthians 13:1-8 (a) (NASB)

If I speak with the tongues of men and of angels but do not have love, I have become a noisy gong or a clanging cymbal.

If I have the gift of prophecy and know all mysteries and all knowledge; and if I have all faith, so as to remove mountains, but do not have love, I am nothing.

And if I give all my possessions to feed the poor, and if I surrender my body to be burned, but do not have love, it profits me nothing.

Love is patient, love is kind and is not jealous; love does not brag and is not arrogant, does not act unbecomingly;

it does not seek its own, is not provoked, does not take into account a wrong suffered, does not rejoice in unrighteousness, but rejoices with the truth;

bears all things, believes all things, hopes all things, endures all things.

Love never fails;

~~~~~~

This love is a love that gives; it is not always considering what it is going to have, but what it may give for the benefit of the other.
David Martyn Lloyd-Jones (1899-1981)

2. Love on Loan

"Well done good and faithful servant, enter into the joy of your Master." - Jesus

It has been stated by many that we will take nothing out of this life. The old bumper sticker said, "you never see a U-Haul behind a hearse." I know what they mean, but as the years roll by, I am not sure I agree with them.

Each of us has been given a gift from God. Perhaps a stewardship would ring truer. God has given us life. The Creator of all has entrusted to each one of us a measure of time. We are born, we live and we die.

While it is true we will not take any earthly possessions along with us, we will send something ahead of us, and we will give an account of what we did with the gift of life we were given.

Jesus discussed laying up treasure in heaven and it seems like that must be possible. I don't think Jesus was thinking about gold, jewels or money, for heaven's streets and walls are paved with the stuff. Since it seems like heaven has enough of those items, what was Jesus referring to?

Jesus told parables about talents and money. What was His point? Was it simply about being a good money manager or was it deeper? While thinking about those parables, did the amount matter or what was done with it? Some received many talents and others less. Did the number given matter or what was done with them?

When we leave this life, we will present back to our Creator the results of our stewardship – give an account. I don't know exactly what will take place, but I think we will say something like, "Here are the results of what I did with my life." If you are like me, that sentence sends a shiver down the spine!

While the Scripture speaks of the Judgment Seat of Christ in 2 Corinthians 5:10:

> For we must all appear before the judgment seat of Christ, so that each one may receive what is due for what he has done in the body, whether good or evil.

this is different than being judged for our sins. Those sins were dealt with at the cross and we are those that have our names written in the Lamb's Book of Life! We are now the righteousness of God in Christ:

> For our sake he made him to be sin who knew no sin
> so that in him we might become the righteousness of
> God. 2 Corinthians 5:21

I do not live in any fear about my eternal condition or judgment; Jesus paid it all for me and I now stand pure and holy because of the Cross! I am viewed through the Blood of Jesus and seen as righteous. What an exchange!

What we will be discussing at the judgment seat of Christ, I believe, will involve the details regarding our stewardship of the life we have been given. What type of return did we present back to our Master? I believe we will give an accounting of the gifts and talents we have been given. In this sense then, I do believe we take something out of this life! Not money, wealth or possessions, but what we have done with what we have been given – our life!

Again, that may cause some fear to rise in our minds but fear not! God has not given us a spirit of fear, but of power, love and a sound mind – 2 Timothy 1:7. Also, John shares this truth with us:

> There is no fear in love, but perfect love casts out fear.
> For fear has to do with punishment, and whoever fears
> has not been perfected in love. 1 John 4:18

We are loved perfectly by perfect Love. I believe this time before the judgement seat of Jesus will be one of explanation, not condemnation. We are dearly loved children of our Father. Even if there is a loss here at the throne, it will be bathed in perfect love.

Since none of us are perfect, of course, there will be works that we have accomplished that did not produce good fruit. Only Jesus is perfect and the rest of us are all in varying stages of being a mess! Jesus knows this and I don't believe we will be condemned for being less than perfect.

My picture of this time is one of Jesus gently unwrapping all of the issues in our life. He will unfold what He was doing and why. All the unanswered questions will be explained and Jesus will drop the veil behind what He was doing. As He shows us His hand in all of those trials, heartaches, failures, and sins, we will fall on our knees and worship Him!

Beyond the failures of this life, I believe we will be given insight into the insignificant. Each of us spends the vast majority of our time just doing the daily things. We have no idea of how God uses all of our small faithful actions.

For example, think of Ruth the Moabite. Ruth decided to follow her mother-in-law back to Israel. A small decision, yet a major one in light of what follows.

Ruth faithfully gleaned day after day in a field. Nothing significant there, for many poor people did the same thing. Yet, if Ruth had not been doing the insignificant the hugely significant act of Boaz seeing her would not have happened.

If Ruth would not have followed her mother-in-law's instructions she would not have married Boaz and would not have been in the blood line of Jesus the Savior of the world.

At the Judgement Seat of Christ, I believe the light of revelation will enter the dark places in our minds and hearts and we will see behind the curtain. We will understand what was really going on from heaven's point of view as we walked out our seemingly insignificant earthly life.

We do not have to live in dread or fear of being examined by the King of Love. In fact, if we are walking with Jesus, and really trying to live a life worthy of His calling, this time will be one of joy and anticipation, not shame and guilt.

I know this to be true for John explains in this verse a marvelous truth:

> By this is love perfected with us, so that we may have confidence for the day of judgment, because as he is so also are we in this world. 1 John 4:17

My God loves me and He loves you. He loved me while I hated Him and He loves me now. My God is not waiting to beat me up or to hurt me but is for me. God wants me to succeed and He wants the same for you. You and I can have confidence in the day of judgment because we are loved by Love Himself.

We Are Dearly Loved:

We are dearly loved for a reason and while we may not know all of it, we do know that part of the reason includes freely giving away the love we have received. Consider this sampling of verses:

> A new commandment I give to you, that you love one another: just as I have loved you, you also are to love one another. By this, all people will know that you are my disciples if you have love for one another."
> John 13:34-35

This is my commandment, that you love one another as I have loved you. John 15:12

Owe no one anything, except to love each other, for the one who loves another has fulfilled the law. Romans 13:8

Having purified your souls by your obedience to the truth for a sincere brotherly love, love one another earnestly from a pure heart, 1 Peter 1:22

Above all, keep loving one another earnestly, since love covers a multitude of sins. 1 Peter 4:8

Paul, John, Peter, and Jesus all stated that we are to love others with the love we have received. In fact, Jesus commanded us to love. Love is not a feeling, and we will further define love later, but for now, we are loved deeply by our Father so that we can turn around and love others.

We will learn to love others because the King of Love resides in our heart. We have been loved, and therefore we will love. We must. John is so sure of this that he states the following:

Whoever says he is in the light and hates his brother is still in darkness. 1 John 2:9

By this it is evident who are the children of God, and who are the children of the devil: whoever does not practice righteousness is not of God, nor is the one who does not love his brother. 1 John 3:10

> We know that we have passed out of death into life
> because we love the brothers. Whoever does not
> love abides in death. 1 John 3:14

> If anyone says, "I love God," and hates his brother,
> he is a liar; for he who does not love his brother
> whom he has seen cannot love God whom he has
> not seen. 1 John 4:20

We know we are in the Light, we are a child of God, we have passed into life, and we are in the truth because we love others. The opposite is also true. Hate reveals that we are not in the light, we are a child of the devil, still in death and a liar. God simply will not allow any child of His to dwell in anything but love. It is a process and a destination, but rest assured, if we know Jesus, we will reach it.

We have been given a gift of life and love. God expects each of His children to produce a return on that investment. At least part of the expected return is to learn how to walk in love towards others. We are to demonstrate what real, God-love looks like to those around us.

We can love because we are loved. In fact, God requires us to love those around us as an outward expression of an inward reality. If we have really encountered Love Himself, then we will love others. We cannot help it!

Love Fulfills the Law:

I do not want to start a debate over law and grace, yet, I can't help but at least mention these two encounters within God's Word. One day Jesus was approached by the

religious rulers that were seeking to entrap Him. In
Matthew 22:35-40 we find the account of the discussion:

> And one of them, a lawyer, asked him a question to
> test him. "Teacher, which is the great commandment
> in the Law?" And he said to him, "You shall love the
> Lord your God with all your heart and with all your
> soul and with all your mind. This is the great and
> first commandment. And a second is like it: You shall
> love your neighbor as yourself. On these two
> commandments depend all the Law and the
> Prophets."

We all know that loving God is primary, but Jesus went
beyond that requirement and added for free the second
greatest commandment – love your neighbor as yourself!
That reply would have been shocking to the self-loving
religious leaders. The men Jesus shared this with despised
others and rejected anyone that didn't measure up to their
standards.

Jesus pointed out that the second commandment was
like the first one and that is interesting. Jesus seemed to
be stating that how we loved others was an outworking of
the Law and Prophets, which was a common way to
describe the Old Testament writings in Jesus' day.

At least part of the Law and Prophets was written to
actually impact how people treated others. Sometimes it is
easy for me to lose sight of why all those laws were written,
but for our purposes, Jesus is expressing how important
loving our neighbors really is.

If that was not shocking enough, Paul further reduces
and clarifies the question asked to Jesus with this thought:

> For the whole law is fulfilled in one word: "You shall love your neighbor as yourself."
> Galatians 5:14

This sentence is indeed staggering because Paul leaves out loving God and only focuses on loving others as the fulfillment of the Law. Did Paul really mean that how we love others is the one word to fulfill the whole Law? How do you read it?

If you couple Paul's thoughts with John's that I have spread throughout the book, it is clear that how we walk in love is extremely important and defines what has taken place within our hearts through salvation.

It would seem that God wants us to learn how to walk in love, both receiving His, and then passing that love along to others in our journey through this life.

Before we move to consider why God has done some of the things He has done, let's pause a few minutes and prayerfully consider some questions.

For Our Consideration:

1. What does stewardship mean to you, and specifically regarding our earthly lives?

2. What do you think some of the treasure is that Jesus commands us to lay up in heaven?

3. I explained mine, but what is your picture of standing before Jesus at His judgment seat?

4. Why was John so clear regarding love, hate and how they interact revealing our relationship with God?

1 Corinthians 13:1-8 (a) (KJV)

Though I speak with the tongues of men and of angels and have not charity, I am become as sounding brass or a tinkling cymbal.

And though I have the gift of prophecy, and understand all mysteries, and all knowledge; and though I have all faith, so that I could remove mountains, and have not charity, I am nothing.

And though I bestow all my goods to feed the poor, and though I give my body to be burned, and have not charity, it profiteth me nothing.

Charity suffereth long, and is kind; charity envieth not; charity vaunteth not itself, is not puffed up,

Doth not behave itself unseemly, seeketh not her own, is not easily provoked, thinketh no evil;

Rejoiceth not in iniquity, but rejoiceth in the truth; Beareth all things, believeth all things, hopeth all things, endureth all things.

Charity never faileth:

~~~~~~

Christ loved the church, His spouse, although there were many spots, blemishes, and imperfections in Her. He loved her, better than Himself and His own life, and shed His most precious blood for her. Ezekiel Hopkins (1634-1690)

3. God Forced Love

Accept the one whose faith is weak, without quarreling over disputable matters. Romans 14:1

God loved us and now we must learn to love others. John and Jesus both said that if we love others, this will be our calling card to those desperately needing the glorious Good News of the Gospel.

Sadly, the Church is not known for love. The Bride of Christ is known for many things, like greed, complaining, division, disunity, sexual failures, and did I mention begging for money? But loving others is not often used by those outside of the church expressing their view of Her.

The deceiver that tricked Eve is still at work in our day. While eating fruit is not the issue, the method is still the same - get God's people to disobey God's commands and therefore render them ineffective.

Love is a Command:

Jesus is clear:

A new commandment I give to you, that you love one another: just as I have loved you, you also are to love one another. John 13:34

This is my commandment, that you love one another as I have loved you. John 15:12

These things I command you so that you will love one another. John 15:17

If you love me, you will keep my commandments. John 14:15

The enemy of our souls has been successful in causing the Church to disobey His direct command to walk in love one towards another, and frankly, it is not really debatable. The Church is more known for shooting their wounded and for fighting than known for loving one another.

The command to love others did not originate in the New Testament. Some try to prove that the Old Testament God is different than the One revealed in the New, but consider this passage from Leviticus 19:17-18:

You shall not hate your brother in your heart, but you shall reason frankly with your neighbor, lest you incur sin because of him. You shall not take vengeance or bear a grudge against the sons of your own people, but you shall love your neighbor as yourself: I am the Lord.

It seems that even in the Old Testament, God was concerned about how His people interacted with one another. Reason frankly, do not take vengeance upon, do not keep a grudge, and love instead. Why? Because I am the Lord! If we know the Lord we will learn to walk in love towards others. We simply cannot help it.

The reality we face is that there are thousands of denominations and Christians have caused death and destruction down through the centuries. Splits, divisions, power plays, and every manner of sinful behavior have been and are still being performed in the churches of our day. The Church stands condemned in Her failure to walk in obedience to Jesus clear command – love one another!

While you may disagree with me over the degree of what was just written, just ask any passerby on the street what the Church of Jesus Christ is known for, and love will probably not be the first answer, and that is a real shame.

Jesus commanded us to love, yet we often fail miserably. We will explore some reasons why later, but for now, we must understand that love is not a feeling, but a choice. If love was simply an emotion or feeling, God would be unjust in commanding us to love others. I cannot force or command a feeling. I can, however, choose to walk in Biblical love.

Before we define love in detail, let me ask you a question – why did God allow the Bible to be written the way it is? Sixty-six books, multiple authors, a compilation of history, poetry, letters, and even strange visionary type language.

Not to be disrespectful or come across as an arrogant preacher, but if absolute clarity and uniformity were the desire, then the Bible fails. There are thousands of denominations, a long history of church councils convened, blood spilled, and division still runs rampant over whether we even have free will. Good people read the same Book and disagree over:

- Water baptism
- Communion
- Church government
- Worship and music
- The Holy Spirit
- Salvation
- End times
- Role of Israel
- Sabbath
- Theological Grids
- _____Fill in your favorite hot topic here

Why didn't God simply provide us with clear instructions regarding these and dozens of other divisive ones? Why didn't God instruct Paul to add a chapter here or there and clear up these issues? How hard would have been for God to have a chapter on church government, how to conduct a wedding or funeral, or exactly how one should conduct a worship service?

If God was after explicit instructions to end division, then the Bible was poorly written. I think we all agree that God could have had it written any way He desired, so He did not make a mistake. If that thought is true, then He had a reason for providing us the Scriptures in the fashion He did. Is it that God just loves to see His children argue and bicker? Is it that God enjoys conflict?

While I can't claim to know all the answers, I would put forth one suggested reason – God presented the Scriptures in their current format so that His children would learn to walk in Biblical love. Anyone can love those that agree with them, but the type of love God was after requires overlooking, endurance, patience, the extending of grace, willingness to yield, humility, etc., and these are birthed in differences of opinion. God wants His children to learn how to love those that don't agree with us, and this takes a different kind of love – a Biblical love.

Love Defined:

We are given God's definition of love in 1 Corinthians 13:4-7 and most of us can quote it or read it on a plaque in our homes and you have already seen it a few times in this book:

> Love is patient and kind; love does not envy or boast; it is not arrogant or rude. It does not insist on its own way; it is not irritable or resentful; it does not rejoice at wrongdoing but rejoices with the truth. Love bears all things, believes all things, hopes all things, endures all things.

This type of love, agape in the Greek, God-given, grace-activated, and others focused love comes from Love Himself into His people. We are given the Holy Spirit at salvation and from that moment on, we can, and I would argue, must learn to walk in love towards others.

Even a casual reading of the verses above will cause the reader to reflect on what love is and is not from Paul's point of view. Love is not an emotion but a choice. This type love has little to do with feelings and everything to do with our decisions. We love because we want to obey our Lord's clear command. When we do not love others, it is not because we can't; we choose not to.

As we observed in the first part of this chapter, Jesus commanded love from His followers towards others. How can this be if love is a feeling or emotion? You cannot command someone to feel or experience joy, sadness, mercy or pleasure. You can command someone to make a choice and Biblical love is, therefore, a choice.

Choosing to be patient or kind is a choice. Choosing to not get even or boast is a choice. Choosing not to be arrogant or rude is a choice. Choosing to not insist on our own way, or to be irritable or resentful are all choices. Choosing not to rejoice in evil or wrongdoing but seeking and enjoying truth are choices. Do we get the point? We make a choice about what we will do and how we will do it.

Paul even goes a bit further to state that not only is love a choice, but it is the best choice. What else is there that will bear, believe, hope and endure all things? Paul unashamedly states that love does.

A few verses later in the chapter Paul adds that love never ends, and in vs. 13 he states, - So now faith, hope, and love abide, these three; but the greatest of these is love.

Faith and hope are wonderful, powerful, necessary and Biblical words, yet Paul elevates love above the other two. We are not only called to love others, we are commanded to do so.

Back to my question about why the Bible was written the way it was instead of more like an instruction manual providing step-by-step details on controversial topics. Perhaps God allowed the Scriptures to be written the way they were so we would learn how to choose to love others as commanded.

Maybe God decided that by writing Truth in such a fashion, His children would have to choose to love those that honestly disagree over the application.

- Will we be patient with other believers that worship using a different style than we enjoy?
- Will we be kind to those that hold to a different view of end times, church government or how to administrate a gathering of believers?
- Will we cease from being envious of successful ministries or boasting about the size of our own crowd?
- Will we embrace humility instead of being rude towards others?
- Will we allow others to hold differing opinions on matters not clearly defined in Scripture?
- Will we learn to rejoice with those that rejoice and weep with those that weep?
- Will we stand for truth and rejoice when truth prevails?
- Will we bear, believe, hope and endure all things related to the Church?

If we will do these things, then we are walking in love. If we really become good at doing these things, maybe the world around the Church will sit up and take notice. Perhaps the world will even know we are His disciples if we learn how to love others.

Jesus commanded His followers to love others. Jesus even went so far as to explain that if we really do, we will provide an indisputable evidence of the reality of the Savior. Perhaps God allowed our wonderful Book to be written the way it is so that we will have ample opportunity to grow in love towards others.

The fact is that God commanded us to love one another. If we really are believers in Jesus Christ as our Savior and Lord, then we have no choice but to learn how to accomplish the primary task assigned.

If loving others is a choice then we must choose differently than our history reveals. The Church is known for far too many things other than love and that is a sad indictment on Her.

We must begin to correct this course in the future if the entire world is to know we are His disciples. Love must take the place of hate, arguments, jealously, unforgiveness, anger, power struggles, and all manner of relational failures.

God actually expects His people to walk in love or He would not have commanded it. When we fail to do so, not only are we disobedient to His revealed will, but we discredit the power and reality of salvation. If the outworking in our daily lives is not love, then the Gospel has failed to produce the results intended by God; the fault is not with the Gospel but with us.

We are supposed to be born again, new creations in Christ. We are now filled with Holy Spirit and empowered to live a new life. This new life will be manifested first and foremost by how we walk with others.

We now have all the power we need to choose love. We can learn to walk in love even towards, and perhaps especially with those that disagree with us. This action will speak far louder than anything else we can do.

Before we move on to look at where most of us learn about love, please pause and think about the following questions.

For Our Consideration:

1. Why do you think Jesus commanded His followers to love another?

2. Why do you think God allowed the Holy Scripture to be written as it is?

3. Are there any areas in your life where love is lacking? What can you do about it?

4. If you were defining love, how would you do it?

1 Corinthians 13:1-8 (a) (NIV)

If I speak in the tongues of men or of angels but do not have love, I am only a resounding gong or a clanging cymbal.

If I have the gift of prophecy and can fathom all mysteries and all knowledge, and if I have a faith that can move mountains, but do not have love, I am nothing.

If I give all I possess to the poor and give over my body to hardship that I may boast, but do not have love, I gain nothing.

Love is patient, love is kind. It does not envy, it does not boast, it is not proud.

It does not dishonor others, it is not self-seeking, it is not easily angered, it keeps no record of wrongs.

Love does not delight in evil but rejoices with the truth. It always protects, always trusts, always hopes, always perseveres.

Love never fails.

~~~~~~

To effect her (the church) redemption, Jesus does not merely employ the operations of His power and of His wisdom but surrendered Himself into the hands of divine justice that, as a sacrifice of atonement, He might ransom the object of His regard at the price of His blood.
John Angell James (1785-1859)

4. Family is the Seedbed for Love

"The family – that dear octopus from whose tentacles we never quite escape, nor, in our inmost hearts, ever quite wish to." Dodie Smith

God saw that it was not good for man to be alone (Genesis 2:18) and so He created a companion. The fact that man was alone did not surprise God for He always knew what He was going to do – create woman. The two were introduced and love, bliss, and joy followed forevermore. Well, we know that is not how the story unfolds, but we can dream about what could have been!

What actually happened was there was an unspecified amount of time during which the happy couple worked and lived in love and peace in God's perfect garden.

One day, the devil in the shape of a serpent showed up and introduced lies and poison about God and love took a major hit that we are still suffering from. We don't know if that was the first conversation or the only time temptation was presented; we do know that on that day it was successful. A wrong choice was made that would impact the rest of human history.

Death was introduced as well as deception, competition, and relational destruction. God's perfect couple would experience pain, suffering, decay and ultimately death. These realities were now going to be handed down for all who followed.

Every marriage now starts in a hole. Even Christian couples still struggle with the death unleashed in the Garden. This is not meant to be a theological discussion over original sin, but simply to make sure we understand that we still have an enemy and we still battle the ravages of the first sin unleashed. We know that Jesus is the Second Adam (1 Corinthians 15:45) and now victory is possible, but, every marriage still carries the scars of that first choice.

We All have a Family:

In our discussion centering on love, marriage, family and these relationships must be considered. Most of us had a family and were not raised by wolves like Mowgli of *Jungle Book* fame. Even those left on the doorstep of an institution had some sort of family. There are many that were adopted or were placed into a series of temporary homes, but all of us have some idea of what family means, even if it was only an image presented in a movie or novel.

We must remember that God came up with the idea of family. He didn't have to. Being infinite in creativity, God could have designed companionship, the birthing of children, and the fulfillment of His command to fill the world with people through many other means.

God could have designed us to function alone. We could have been self-reproducing not needing the opposite sex. Children could have been found hanging from trees like ripe fruit, or perhaps dug out of the ground like carrots.

Whatever could have been is an interesting rabbit trail, but we know what ended up being God's choice. One man marries one woman and through a physical relationship, children are conceived.

Parents are given the task of rearing children, hopefully training them along the line to become mature men and women ready to repeat the cycle.

There are many excellent books on marriage and child training so that is not the purpose of this chapter. My goal is for us to discover the opportunities for love within the confines of the family unit.

We know from experience that men are attracted to women and visa-versa. Most of us that are married at one time dearly loved the one we married. In performing dozens of wedding ceremonies, never has a couple stood before me to state their vows of hate. They have all vowed to love one another unto death. We also know the statistics clearly reveal that many violate those terms prematurely.

What happened from the altar to the divorce court? How could a couple that stood in front of someone like me, and often many other witnesses, boldly proclaiming their love, soon end up despising the person?

There are many reasons of course, but at the root of many marriage issues, is a lack of Biblical love. While 1 Corinthians 13 may be hanging on plaques all over the house, the couple forgot to practice what is written on them.

Patience, kindness, bearing with, and enduring seem to go by the wayside quickly. What once was attractive and even cute, becomes a constant irritant. Many times, opposites attract, yet end up repelling each other in the end.

One mistake many of us make is wasting so much time and energy trying to change our mate into us. If they would simply see the issues, decisions, and way to do things from the correct point of view, i.e. mine, life would be great! We try to change the other person into a clone of ourselves and we end up missing so much in the process.

God did not create duplicate people. Each of us is a unique expression of our Maker. Each of us has value, worth, and a great deal to offer to our world. In marriage, God brings together two people that are vastly different - physically, emotionally, mentally and in personality, not to torture us, but to help us grow in love.

When we quit fighting the differences and learn to embrace them as a gift from God, we will grow, mature, and quite possibly learn to love.

Here is a hard truth that any counselor will tell you — you cannot change the other person, you can only change yourself. God wants us to love our spouse with Agape love. Since this love is a choice, the question is, will we do it? Will we choose to love the person that we promised to love on our wedding day?

I understand that there are circumstances where it becomes impossible to stay and we should flee – abuse, criminal behavior, the other spouse quits and refuses to try, etc. but again, we are responsible for our behavior, not theirs. As far as it depends on us, and as long as it is possible, my question remains – will we choose to walk in agape love towards our spouse?

God provides us many opportunities to grow in love within our own homes. We will be given multiple chances to be patient, kind, to endure, to seek the best for, and to walk out each of love's attributes in our homes. Will we though? Love is a choice commanded by Love Himself.

Marriages that not only survive but thrive, are growing in love, Biblical love. Two are better than one when both are trying to actually walk in love. The world will take notice of Jesus' disciples when they walk in love, and this is true in marriage. With marriages breaking down, falling apart, and with many simply living in a truce, a couple that actually is trying to love one another stands out.

I firmly believe that God designed marriage as a tool to help us grow in our faith and in agape love. We are given choices every day of our marriage to choose love. If your marriage is struggling, re-read 1 Corinthians 13 and think through how you can implement it. What would happen in your marriage if you really did try to love your spouse with no strings attached? I hope you will find out.

Is it really possible to change? Can we make the hard choice to die to ourselves and live for another? What if we make the choice yet our spouse doesn't? Does that even matter? We are responsible for our choices, actions, and reactions; not those of our spouse. What will we choose this day?

Perhaps it is too hard to implement every aspect of love as described by Paul, so choose just one to work on. Pick patience or kindness and try to be so towards your mate. Begin slowly. Overlook an offense or harsh word. Do not return evil for evil when treated rudely. Try to live out the Golden Rule (Matthew 7:12) for an hour. Treat your spouse the way you want to be treated.

Also, consider some of these passages in light of this discussion:

- A soft answer turns away wrath, but a harsh word stirs up anger. Proverbs 15:1

- Do nothing from selfish ambition or conceit but in humility count others more significant than yourselves. Philippians 2:3

- Good sense makes one slow to anger, and it is his glory to overlook an offense. Proverbs 19:11

- Let all bitterness and wrath and anger and clamor and slander be put away from you, along with all malice. Ephesians 4:31

Trying lowering your voice instead of raising it and see if the discussion changes. Does Paul really want us to do *nothing* from selfish ambition? Sure, seems to read that way to me.

Are we supposed to show good sense? Slowing down our responses of anger must be a key. What does overlooking an offense mean? Don't I have to point out the failure instantly if I see it? How are they ever going to grow if I overlook that offense? Perhaps God can show them without you or I pointing it out!

Did Paul really mean all bitterness, wrath, anger, clamor, and slander? Really, all of it? What does Paul expect me to do when I am hurt, wounded, offended, overlooked, and not appreciated? Does Paul really mean that we should simply give grace and understand?

Of course, we must learn to talk through hurtful situations, but we do not have to go to anger, bitterness, etc. We can choose to walk in love, grace, mercy compassion, understanding, and give to our spouse the grace we give to ourselves. We must if we are to learn how to walk in Biblical love.

There are many other such passages, but those few are enough to make my point. We need to treat our spouse with love, grace, mercy, respect, as we would want to be treated. If we can't do everything, we certainly can choose to do something. A small beginning is much better than camping in anger, bitterness and hurt.

No decision is a decision. If we refuse to try then we will never know what could have been different. We must begin somewhere in our journey to learn how to walk in love, and our marriages are an excellent place to begin.

We cannot change our mate, but we certainly can ask the Lord to help change us. We can try and we can choose. Will we?

Children:

Children add multiple opportunities for love to grow. We embrace that cute little bundle of joy and our hearts melt over every little smile and gurgle. Soon, those gurgles start to keep us up at night. The smiles turn into cries from rashes, sickness, and selfish behaviors.

Our adorable little babies become mobile, sometimes defiant, and many of us discover temptations to anger we didn't even know existed. The Scriptures state that children are a blessing, but sometimes parents really wonder about those verses!

Why did God decide that parents should be responsible for raising children? Why were we not simply born fully mature? Besides the obvious physical reasons, God could have had us grown in the garden instead of the womb. He did not choose to do so, therefore, there must be a good reason for God's choice.

Re-reading the definition of love, we certainly can see God's wisdom in giving us our children. Children are wonderful at providing opportunities for parents to grow in patience, kindness, bearing with others, and enduring.

God gives parents a love for their children that must be maintained through the difficult task of training them. God told His people, "Don't desire the death of your son," (Proverbs 19:18), and some of us know what that means! Children can bring out the worst in our thoughts, words, and behaviors.

God gives us children not to torment us, but to help us grow in love. Repeat after me, God gives us our children to help us grow in love. Say this often and we might actually grow to believe it! God didn't have to create the family the way He did, so He must have His reasons.

There are many reasons for God choosing the system He did, including knowing that He would reveal Himself to His creation as Father and that Jesus would be His Son. The family model was chosen because each of us is part of a family and the very mention of the word should provoke thoughts of love.

Perhaps you are one that didn't grow up in a loving family. Your skin begins to crawl whenever the word father or mother is used. Images of abuse, neglect, or hate rise within you. You are not alone.

Still, God came up with the idea of family, the titles involved and the concepts intended. Just because sin and sinners have trashed the terms for us does not mean the concepts are evil or wrong. God is redemptive! God can heal wounds and restore what has been violated. God wants to redeem the family. Maybe He will use you to begin to do so in your world. He is in mine.

God designed love to be first experienced in the family environment. Our enemy hates the family and of course, he assaults it in hopes of destroying it. He can't, nor will he ever be able to do so. We are part of the family of God, heading to an eternal wedding feast and described as the Bride of Christ! No matter how hard the devil, man or sin has tried to destroy the family, God simply will not allow it.

The family unit is the first and best place to discover what love is all about. The family is the place where we can grow in love, even if those around us fail. Love is a choice, and for most of us, it is the family where we first are given the chance to make the decision to walk in love.

As our family grows, ages and multiplies, the opportunity for Agape love expands. Teens have friends. Young adults grow up, marry and introduce another set of potential love objects called in-laws. If God so chooses, grandchildren arrive and the cycle begins to repeat.

At age forty-two I became a grandpa. Now, past sixty-two, and thirteen grandchildren later, I am learning what that word means and how much impact we can have, not only on our children but on their children. What a delight to interact with grown children and growing grandchildren in love. Our influence can span generations, and it should.

God's design for the family is flawless even though man, sin and the devil have attempted to scar it, redefine it, and break it. The family has and will endure for it was God's primary choice of training for new humans.

If we hope for revival, a changing of culture, and long-term stability, we must begin to walk in love in our homes. The enemy has been successful in destroying the family unit, and yet, the restoration of the family will spread out redemption over the world. Of course, redemption is in Christ alone, but the family is the perfect seedbed for revival.

Our first taste of love begins in the family and many of our defining traits are developed in our early years. The world system understands this far better than the Church and has worked overtime to get the children away from the parents as quickly as possible.

If we really want to change our world, we must begin in the home. We begin by learning how to love our spouse, our children, and all of those that are connected via the family unit.

Most of us know that the main reason children reject the Gospel is because they have experienced hypocrisy in the home, meaning, parents that pretend to be one way in Church and live a different way at home.

Children need to see the reality of Christ and not just some words that mean nothing. Every family and every couple have relational issues, but children need to observe godly parents that rely upon Christ to help them walk through the troubles.

Hypocrisy does not mean we don't struggle, it means that we actually live our lives at home in the same way we live them in public. We are not pretenders, but those trying to follow the Scriptures with a truthful heart. We are consistent, not perfect. If children see that the Gospel didn't make any difference in their parent's life and relationship, then why would they want to adopt it for themselves?

If children see imperfect parents attempt to walk in Biblical love practicing forgiveness, giving grace, and crying out to God for help, it is not weakness they see, but reality. Children need to know that God is real and that He can and will help – parents are the primary example of these truths.

Before we move on into other relationships, let's consider our definition of love again from 1 Corinthians 13:4-7 and ask some questions about our family.

- Will we attempt to extend patience and kindness to those in our family even when they irritate us?
- Will we cease to boast and envy others within our homes, putting away jealousy and unhealthy competition?
- Will we not give in to being rude and full of pride toward our family members?
- Will we watch our words and jokes about each other?
- Will we cease demanding our own way and not be resentful when others get theirs?

- Will we not laugh at or enjoy seeing other family members get in trouble or even being blamed for our actions by mistake?
- Will we always attempt to walk in truth one towards another?
- Will we bear, believe, hope, and endure whatever may come our way together as a family?

These "will we" questions maybe don't seem like much, but each reflect a choice we can make. My appeal is this – what would happen if we really did try to respond in love in our homes?

For Our Consideration:

1. Why do you think the family is under such assault in our day?

2. In thinking about your childhood, what would you change if you could?

3. How would living out 1 Corinthians 13 actually change your marriage and family?

4. Is there one choice you could make today to change the direction of your family?

1 Corinthians 13:1-8 (a) (HCSB)

If I speak human or angelic languages but do not have love, I am a sounding gong or a clanging cymbal.

If I have the gift of prophecy and understand all mysteries and all knowledge, and if I have all faith so that I can move mountains but do not have love, I am nothing.

And if I donate all my goods to feed the poor, and if I give my body in order to boast but do not have love, I gain nothing.

Love is patient, love is kind. Love does not envy, is not boastful, is not conceited, does not act improperly, is not selfish, is not provoked, and does not keep a record of wrongs. Love finds no joy in unrighteousness but rejoices in the truth.

It bears all things, believes all things, hopes all things, endures all things.

Love never ends.

~~~~~~

It is worthy of special notice that, in all the apostolic injunctions, the great duty enforced upon the husband is love...It is with some surprise that we find it set home upon the conscience of the husband as his paramount obligation...this command to love.
Benjamin M. Palmer (1818-1903)

5. Church is a Place to Learn Love

For where God built a church, there the Devil would also build a chapel. Martin Luther

Ah, the Church! The place where the saints gather around the throne to worship the Lord in the beauty of holiness. What a sight from heaven's point of view. There are great mysteries surrounding the Church and her gatherings.

Consider these passage as we begin our discussion:

- And I tell you, you are Peter, and on this rock, I will build my church, and the gates of hell shall not prevail against it. Matthew 16:18

51

- To me, though I am the very least of all the saints, this grace was given, to preach to the Gentiles the unsearchable riches of Christ, and to bring to light for everyone what is the plan of the mystery hidden for ages in God, who created all things, so that through the church the manifold wisdom of God might now be made known to the rulers and authorities in the heavenly places.
  Ephesians 3:8-10

- And when he had taken the scroll, the four living creatures and the twenty-four elders fell down before the Lamb, each holding a harp, and golden bowls full of incense, which are the prayers of the saints. Revelation 5:8

Jesus said He would build His church. Paul stated that the manifold wisdom of God would now be made known to all in the heavenly realms through the church. John gives a glimpse of what happens to the prayers of the church, and these three passages are just the beginning of the glory and mystery of the church.

The church, the gathering of the saints of God, should be a place of a clear demonstration of love, but is it? If the world will know we are Jesus' disciples by our love, why is love not the defining attribute of every gathering of the witness on earth known as the church?

The opening quote in this chapter from Luther is at least part of the answer. Wherever two or more are gathered, the Lord is indeed in the midst of them, but then so is the enemy.

Matthew 13 reveals two parables that certainly could apply to this discussion. The first one is the Sower and the Seed presented in verses 1-23. We know the story very well, so I will just glance over the end. As Jesus explains the parable to His disciples, the punch line is that even the good seed will yield varying results. My translation? Even good people do not love perfectly. We are growing and learning, but perfection is yet to be achieved.

The Parable of the Weeds is presented in verses 24-30. A man plants his field and an enemy under the cover of darkness sowed weeds among the good seeds. It is not readily apparent until time passes that the weeds are there. The owner instructs his servants to allow the weeds to grow alongside the seeds until the harvest and then he will destroy them at the right time. My translation? There will always be fake believers among the real ones.

In both of these stories, Jesus reveals the need for love. We must learn to love those that are stronger and those that are weaker. We must learn to love our enemies and learn to love the other church family members. We can and must learn how to love in the Church.

Struggling to love one another within the church is not new. In fact, much of the New Testament was written to assist the Church in figuring out how to do just that.

- I appeal to you, brothers, by the name of our Lord Jesus Christ, that all of you agree, and that there be no divisions among you, but that you be united in the same mind and the same judgment.
  1 Corinthians 1:10

- For, in the first place, when you come together as a church, I hear that there are divisions among you. And I believe it in part, 1 Corinthians 11:18

- I entreat Euodia and I entreat Syntyche to agree in the Lord. Yes, I ask you also, true companion, help these women, who have labored side by side with me in the gospel together with Clement and the rest of my fellow workers, whose names are in the book of life. Philippians 4:2-3

- And there arose a sharp disagreement so that they separated from each other. Barnabas took Mark with him and sailed away to Cyprus, Acts 15:39

- But when Cephas came to Antioch, I opposed him to his face, because he stood condemned. Galatians 2:11

Paul had to appeal to the gathering in Corinth due to the divisions taking place among them. Camps were being chosen and preferred leaders were being idolized. Division and strife naturally follow and the reputation of Christ takes a direct hit because of His people. Lack of love among the Bride reflects poorly upon the Groom.

I don't know who the ladies were that Paul addressed in Philippi, but he appealed to them and to the rest of the church body to help them get along with one another.

I always marvel at the story in Acts 15. How do you not flow and work together with a guy nicknamed "Son of Encouragement?" I'm not sure, but Paul and Barnabas argued so strongly that they couldn't work together any longer. The issue of disagreement centered on a young man named Mark. This again makes me think of relationship difficulties.

Whatever the issue between Paul, Barnabas, and Mark, we do know that Mark becomes Peter's, right-hand man, and towards the end of Paul's life, Paul requests Mark's company, and refers to him as valuable to him, (2 Timothy 4:11) thus offering a picture of reconciliation and redemption in the relationships.

Fighting, arguing and being frustrated with others within the Body of Christ is not limited to those sitting in the pews. Paul and Peter had a nasty exchange recorded in the Galatian passage. These two apostolic heavyweights were standing toe-to-toe over hypocrisy. What to do with all these Gentiles becoming Christians was a real issue for the Jewish believers.

Peter became the primary apostle to the Jews, and Paul to the Gentiles. When their paths crossed in Galatia, it was not pretty. The point is not a detailed study of the issues involved, but for us to realize that even apostles can struggle to walk in love one towards another.

By the way, the Gentile issue was such a problem that the entire church leadership had a major shouting match in Acts 15. The issue was settled, but what a meeting that must have been!

There are many such passages within the Scriptures, but these are sufficient to make the point – worshipping with people is no guarantee that we will all get along and walk in love. Just because the King of Love has granted us eternal life does not guarantee that we will avoid all relational issues with His other kids. In fact, it almost assures us we will.

There will always be people that rub us the wrong way as we gather together. The guy that sings so loud, yet off key. Or if you are part of a clapping type church, how about the one that is always on the wrong beat? The lady with the big hat or the one who is always quick to add some harsh comment into every conversation.

There are the gossips, the ones that have to always be in the know about everyone's business, the ones that like to be seen by all, and those with opinions on everything that must be shared with everyone.

Why can't all these people see as clearly as I do? Why can't these people allow me to remove their speck...oh wait, maybe my log is getting in the way – Matthew 7:3.

So, with that quick backdrop, how do we learn to not only get along with others in the Church but actually grow to love one another so the world takes notice? The answer is the same, we must learn how to walk in 1 Corinthians 13 love toward one another. Let me go through each of the attributes of love again and ask us if we will choose to:

- Be patient towards those that disagree with us, are unkind to us, or do not include us in their circle.
- Be kind to those that overlook us, do not give us credit for our work, or proper acknowledgment.
- Ignore the temptation to envy others when they receive praise or attention.
- Not boast about ourselves, or how we serve, or our gifts and talents.
- Reject pride and comparing ourselves to others.
- Go out of our way to look for those that are often overlooked by others.

- Be willing to yield to others for the sake of love and unity.
- Refuse to be irritable when interrupted, ignored, or overlooked.
- Reject resentment when offended instead move quickly to forgiveness.
- Only enjoy what is true, honest, lovely and reject wrongdoing, lies, gossip, and backbiting.
- Bear all things, believe all things, hope all things, and endure all things.

If the believers in a local church actually attempted to do these things would the spirit of the congregation change?

But you don't understand, I am hurt, rejected, overlooked, ignored, wounded, and not happy! While I may not understand all of the details of your situation, the Scripture is clear regarding our response to all of those emotions and wounds – LOVE.

We can choose to forgive and in fact, we must. If we read Matthew 18 and actually believe it, the punch line at the end of the story should produce a healthy fear of unforgiveness:

> Then his master summoned him and said to him, 'You wicked servant! I forgave you all that debt because you pleaded with me. And should not you have had mercy on your fellow servant, as I had mercy on you?' And in anger, his master delivered him to the jailers until he should pay all his debt. So also my heavenly Father will do to every one of you if you do not forgive your brother from your heart. Matthew 18:32-35

What did the master do to the one that wouldn't forgive? Did Jesus really say that His Father would do the same to us if we fail to forgive? I do not see any choice but to forgive those that hurt or wound me.

After the family, the church is the perfect place to safely learn to love others. Yes, there are hypocrites and fakes, but there are also genuine people that need loving. We can grow in love towards others, including the ones only pretending, but we must love, for so we are commanded by the King of Love. The gathering of God's people is a perfect place to grow in love one towards another.

Love is a choice. So is service. If we want to be great in the Kingdom, Jesus said we need to become a servant of all. (Mark 10:43) If we really want to grow in love here is a suggestion – look around for someone to serve. In every church, there are needs. Why don't you fill them if you can? We can't do everything, but we all can do something.

One key to a satisfying life is to serve. It is hard to be self-focused, self-centered, self-absorbed when we are serving others. Every act of kindness, every act of service, no matter how menial we may think it is, is seen by our Father. Jesus came to seek and save the lost. Jesus came to serve and if we want to be more like Him, so should we.

How about taking a few minutes the next time you gather with your local church to look around to see the ones that are alone. There is always someone that is on the outside looking in. Standing alone against the wall or sitting alone at a table. Go up to them and talk. Invite them out to eat or to join your group of friends. Love does that.

If you are that person by yourself, then look around, there are probably others. Instead of worrying about not being included, go include someone else. You might just find a friend for life.

For Our Consideration:

1. Here is an assignment – go through each book of the New Testament and find out why it was written. How many of them are directly dealing with interpersonal problems?

2. Why is it so important to God that His children learn to love one another? Why is it so important to the devil that they don't?

3. Think of the person in your local church that bothers you the most. What attribute of love could you apply to help change your attitude towards that person?

4. Why did Jesus state that being a servant is important to the Kingdom? What did He mean by being a servant?

1 Corinthians 13:1-8 (a) (GNT)

I may be able to speak the languages of human beings and even of angels, but if I have no love, my speech is no more than a noisy gong or a clanging bell.

I may have the gift of inspired preaching; I may have all knowledge and understand all secrets; I may have all the faith needed to move mountains—but if I have no love, I am nothing.

I may give away everything I have, and even give up my body to be burned—but if I have no love, this does me no good.

Love is patient and kind; it is not jealous or conceited or proud; love is not ill-mannered or selfish or irritable; love does not keep a record of wrongs; love is not happy with evil, but is happy with the truth.

Love never gives up; and its faith, hope, and patience never fail.

Love is eternal.

~~~~~~

The Lord Jesus loves His church unselfishly, that is to say, He never loved her for what she has, but what she is. Nay, I must go further than that, and say that He loved her, not so much for what she is, but what He makes her as the object of His love. He loves her not for what comes to Him from her, or with her, but for what He is able to bestow upon her. His is the strongest love that ever was, for He has loved uncomeliness until He has change it into beauty.
C. H. Spurgeon (1834-1892)

6. "But I Am Right"

I'm never wrong, just different levels of right. · Pinterest

One of the reasons we struggle with loving others is that they don't agree with us. I am right. I am right on most issues. What I really mean is I am right on every issue. If you don't see it the same way, then you are wrong. When you begin to see clearly you will agree that I am right. Most of us would not be so brash as to say this out loud, but if we examine our hearts, we will probably find that we believe these things.

How could these sentences not be true? Who willingly holds a wrong opinion on anything? Of course, we believe our view is the correct one, how could we do otherwise? Why would I cling to something that I know to be a lie, false, or inaccurate? I don't so therefore I must be right.

The reality is that we do cling to views, opinions, and facts that are in error or at least allow for someone else to hold a different opinion on the topic and not be wrong. How could we not? We are not God, we are not infallible, and we are not the sum knowledge of all truth and wisdom.

Most of us would agree with my logic so far; we are not God, we cannot know everything, there is strong possibility that I may be in error on something, I could be wrong. I could have blind spots, after all, they are called blind spots because we don't see them.

Why don't we get to this conclusion easier and earlier? Why do we fight with people, our family, spouse, employer, employees, or the referee about their views? Because we believe we are correct. By the way, most others believe they are correct in their views just like we do.

Life has a way of changing our minds. As time passes, what we believe to be true sometimes changes with additional input. Many strongly held views moderate or even are rejected as we age or gain additional insight. At sixteen we may think we know everything and that those parents of ours were pretty dumb. As we pass forty or fifty, we realize that perhaps they were smarter than we thought.

As we marry, have our own children, go to work full time and pay bills, sometimes understanding of our parents grow. Maybe they knew more than we thought they did back when we knew everything there was to know.

God's Word is true and almost everything else is subject to growth, additional information, change, and development – humans included! We age and begin to see that life doesn't always fit into our nice boxes. We encounter people that are different, hold alternate views, and yet, are still good people.

Not everyone has to agree with me, and that is a revelation that sometimes comes slowly.

What is true today was also true in Jesus' day. This story is told of how denominations really started...

Some friends brought a blind man to Jesus to be healed. (Matthew 9) Jesus asked him "Do you believe that I am able to do this?" After the man answered yes, Jesus then gave them the formula to getting blind eyes healed, "According to your faith will it be done to you," Jesus said. Then Jesus touched his eyes and they were opened. All those looking on now "knew" how this eye healing stuff works. You say the formula and place your hands on his eyes. Thus, "The laying on of hands to heal blind people by the formula ministry" was birthed.

Some time later, other people brought another blind man to Jesus. (Mark 8) Jesus gave them the formula of spitting on this man's eyes and placing His hands on him and the man's eyes were opened. Those who watched now knew the formula to open blind eyes. Thus, "The spitting in the eyes of blind people so they can be healed society" was birthed.

Still, later, another blind man was brought to Jesus by another set of folks. (John 9) Those watching saw "Spitting on the ground and making mud to heal eyes society" being birthed.

From this day on the three camps were at odds with each other. Camp A would say "The only proper way to heal blind eyes is by repeating the specific words of our Lord and placing your hands on the blind person's eyes."

"No, no, no," says camp B, "The only spiritual way to heal blind eyes is by spitting on their eyes, any other way is of the devil."

Camp C was shouting by this time, "You must spit on the ground, what kind of insensitive person would spit in the eyes of a poor blind person?" And the fighting has been going on for two thousand years...

Ridiculous, you say? That does not happen today, you mutter. While estimates vary as to the actual number, there are hundreds of denominations, each holding to what they believe to be correct points of view. Why so many?

All of us are tempted to be in one of these three camps in my story. It may not be how to heal blind eyes, but what about:

- Types of worship services/prayer
- TV/movie standards
- Dating or courtship
- Types of education for our children
- How we dress
- How we use our spare time
- How we minister the Gospel
- How we evangelize
- How many children we may or may not have
- Where we go for vacation
- How we spend our money/debt
- What type of house we live in
- Hair length, tattoos
- Social drinking
- Social media usage
- Political issues
- Whether we like sports or not
- How we eat
- _____Fill in our favorite ten or more here

But, I'm right in my opinions and everyone else is entitled to it! There are countless areas that we "judge" each other where God has not asked us to do so. God is very creative and is not limited to our opinions of how someone else's life should be lived.

Just to be clear, I am not talking about sinful matters here, but choices that are clearly outside of the Scripture. If someone is violating the Word of God, we have a different set of choices of how to interact with them. Bearing with them in love still applies, but we cannot and must not ignore sin. If sin is involved, then we follow Matthew 18:15-17, and Galatians 6:1.

What Paul is referring to in the following verse are not sinful matters, but choices that we make that are subject to personal opinions and convictions.

> I have applied all these things to myself and Apollos for your benefit, brothers, that you may learn by us not to go beyond what is written, that none of you may be puffed up in favor of one against another.
> 1 Corinthians 4:6

> As for the one who is weak in faith, welcome him, but not to quarrel over opinions. One person believes he may eat anything, while the weak person eats only vegetables. Let not the one who eats despise the one who abstains and let not the one who abstains pass judgment on the one who eats, for God has welcomed him. Who are you to pass judgment on the servant of another? It is before his own master that he stands or falls. And he will be upheld, for the Lord is able to make him stand. Romans 14:1-4

How easy it is to quarrel over opinions that we don't agree with. Eating meat or vegetables may not be an issue like it was in Paul's day, but pick one off the list just given and see how it goes.

There is very little written in the Scripture about any of the items I listed. Yet, people fight, argue, divide, demean, and pass judgment on one another freely on such matters. Paul said do not despise or pass judgment on the one that disagrees with you. Now, there is an option!

At the end of the Romans section just listed, Paul reveals the truth – the Lord will make sure His own stand! It might be easier if we did not knock out each other's feet all the time while debating over matters that godly people can disagree upon. God often has to pick up others that we have knocked down with our hurtful looks, shunning and words.

Paul explained to the Corinthians that we need to stop at the limits of what is written, and that is excellent advice! If the Scripture is clear then let's be strong, adamant, and take stands upon the truth. If the Scripture gives leeway or is subject to interpretation, then let's not shoot each other in the name of our opinion.

Let love guide us, not the demand that we are the sum total of all truth and answers in debatable matters. We are not. Good people can honestly disagree and still walk in love. We are commanded to love one another and leave the perfecting of one another to God.

When we grow to appreciate the differences in each other instead of criticizing them, we will be maturing in Christ.

Differing Personalities:

Business, sporting teams, and churches often spend a great deal of money attempting to train their employees and volunteers about personality traits.

If you Google the question as to how many personality tests there are available, you will find the most common answer is about 2,500! That should be insightful alone.

Myers-Briggs, DISC, Winslow Personality Profile, and a host of others are offered to provide us with insight to who we are and how we can get along with others that are different from us. Given the fact that there are so many tests, we must assume that we are all a bit different, and this difference is a big deal.

Having taken several of these tests in my life, I know the goal of the test was to identify primary traits, motivations, and even blind spots in myself and how those best interact (or not) with others. I won't bore you with the details, but if you have never taken one, it might be insightful.

In an attempt to explain personality differences an example was given to me as a young believer that has stayed with me all these years.

Picture in your mind a young woman carrying a tray full of dishes walking around a corner into a kitchen. As she rounds the corner she trips over a hole in the carpet and drops the tray. As the embarrassed young lady tries to pick up the mess, also picture four friends around her and their response to her.

Her first friend begins with, "If you would have been more careful, that wouldn't have happened. If you would have not tried to carry so many plates you would have seen the hole and then not tripped making this mess. People never seem to take the time necessary to do the job properly. Just slow down, stack the dishes in the proper formation, and be more observant."

Her second friend gets down on the floor with her and gives her a hug and says, "I'm so sorry you dropped the tray. Don't let them bother you, everyone drops things at times, and it will be okay, let's get this mess cleaned up together. I remember the last time I made a big mess and I just wanted to die, don't worry I will help you and it will all work out, you'll see."

Her third friend begins to bark orders to those around, "You over there, get some towels, and you, tape off this area so no one else slips and falls. We need a trash can, broom, and mop so you there, go get them quickly man, can't you see what is going on here? We need to deal with that hole in the carpet quickly, so get some duct tape."

The final friend begins to instruct those watching on why the event happened. How the dishes were not quite stacked correctly, and why the carpet hole had expanded. "If a mirror is installed right there, then this event could be prevented next time. We need to review the carpet maintenance schedule and perhaps offer some retraining on how to stack dishes on the tray. We can all learn something from this mess if we think about it and don't waste this opportunity."

Now, which one of the friends was correct in their response to the poor girl? Which one was wrong? Which one helped and which one hurt? Your answer will probably depend on your personality type for all of them were correct. They all approached the same situation in a completely different fashion, but each was correct.

In our lives, we will have those that begin to point out what is wrong, went wrong and how we could of and should have prevented it by being more careful. We will also have those that get down into our mess and help us clean it up making sure we are okay emotionally.

We will most likely have those that are organized and producers that will take charge and begin to issue commands to bring order to chaos. And, we will have those that see everything as an opportunity to teach and instruct everyone.

Which one is right? Which one is more important? Which one is not needed? Which one are you? Which one is your spouse? Your children? Your irritating friend? Which one bothers you the most and why do they?

Looking at the strengths of others instead of how they are lacking in whichever one of the four we are, will help us receive from them instead of being frustrated or hurt by them. No two people are exactly alike and each is important.

We can learn from each of these four, but we probably have one we relate to more than others. All are needed and all are correct. If we can learn to slow down our reaction to the differences we might just learn to receive the gifts in each personality type.

We also can and should grow into being more like the other three tendencies and not use our personality traits as an excuse for lack of service, being rude, bossy, or self-focused. The goal of discovering the differences is to become more Christ-like, not less through self-justification of poor behavior.

Now, back to my story about the blind being healed. Jesus was able to heal in many ways, and one was not right and the others wrong. Jesus was able to love a wide variety of people from all walks of life, they did not all have to be the same. The primary requirements Jesus gave to us was to follow Him and to love one another.

Jesus is more than able to build His church and deal with all the problems we see. Jesus is the One that will perfect the saints, bring repentance to those that need it, and conform His followers into His image. We are required to walk in love toward one another during the process.

Let's quit knocking the legs out from under each other by criticizing and putting each other down on debatable matters or because they have a different personality than ours. Instead, let's help one another stand firm in the grace of our Lord Jesus until the day He returns to get us!! After all, there is more than one way to heal a blind man or fix a mess!

So, how does walking in 1 Corinthians 13 type love fit into this discussion? I won't go through the whole list, but how about these to begin your thought process on the matter:

- Will I be patient with someone that chooses to do something (not sinful) I wouldn't do?
- Will I be kind to someone that choose to go somewhere or participate in an activity that I wouldn't?
- Will I refrain from insulting, being rude or arrogant over someone else's non-sinful choices?
- Do I have to insist on my own way being correct?
- Is it possible for someone to disagree with me and still be godly?

You get the idea. We can look at love's attributes and learn how to bear with others, believe in Jesus' ability to reveal truth and error to His other children and allow love to be the greatest choice, even in debatable choices.

For Our Consideration:

1. Why does the Lord allow us to hold wrong opinions and have blind spots?

2. Why is it so easy to judge others that see matters differently than we do?

3. Think about your last conflict with someone and go through love's attributes. What could have been done differently?

4. What strong opinions do you hold that you consider to be immovable and how do you respond to others that hold differing ones?

1 Corinthians 13:1-8 (a) (TLB)

If I had the gift of being able to speak in other languages without learning them and could speak in every language there is in all of heaven and earth, but didn't love others, I would only be making noise.

If I had the gift of prophecy and knew all about what is going to happen in the future, knew everything about everything, but didn't love others, what good would it do? Even if I had the gift of faith so that I could speak to a mountain and make it move, I would still be worth nothing at all without love.

If I gave everything I have to poor people, and if I were burned alive for preaching the Gospel but didn't love others, it would be of no value whatever.

Love is very patient and kind, never jealous or envious, never boastful or proud, never haughty or selfish or rude. Love does not demand its own way. It is not irritable or touchy. It does not hold grudges and will hardly even notice when others do it wrong. It is never glad about injustice but rejoices whenever truth wins out.

If you love someone, you will be loyal to him no matter what the cost. You will always believe in him, always expect the best of him, and always stand your ground in defending him.

All the special gifts and powers from God will someday come to an end, but love goes on forever.

~~~~~~

Jesus gave Himself for her that He might redeem her from all iniquity and purify unto Himself a peculiar people, zealous of good works. His precepts, His prayers, His tears, His blood, His birth, His life, His death, His resurrection His intercession are all for her holiness and purity. His name is called Jesus because He saves His people, not in, but from their sin and unholiness. George Swinnock (1627-1673)

7. Loving Those that Hurt You

From the ends of the earth, we hear songs of praise, of glory to the Righteous One. But I say, "I waste away, I waste away. Woe is me! For the traitors have betrayed, with betrayal the traitors have betrayed." Isaiah 24:16

It is inevitable that hurts will come to us in this life, but sometimes they are over the top painful. A beloved spouse violates their marriage vows. A dearly loved child turns on you and curses you to your face. A friend, that you believed was closer than a brother, is caught spreading lies and gossip about you. These situations, and dozens more like them, are real and they cause a great deal of tears and heartache.

I'm not denying the pain of these type circumstances, but I will challenge us to figure out a way to respond to them in love.

Jesus was betrayed by Judas, rejected by all of the disciples, and Peter denied that he even knew Him three times. All of these would have caused emotional pain and disappointment to the Savior, so, Jesus can relate to us in our pain of rejection perfectly.

> And the Lord turned and looked at Peter. And Peter remembered the saying of the Lord, how he had said to him, "Before the rooster crows today, you will deny me three times." Luke 22:61

Our bloodied, beaten Savior, when He needed support of one of His best friends, was disappointed in the worst way. Can you imagine the look on Jesus' face at that precise moment of Peter's third denial?

My point is not whether Jesus could tell the future, or an attempt to define what Jesus was thinking at that moment, but to guarantee you that our Savior understood our relational pain.

> For because he himself has suffered when tempted, he is able to help those who are being tempted. Hebrews 2:18

> For we do not have a high priest who is unable to sympathize with our weaknesses, but one who in every respect has been tempted as we are, yet without sin. Hebrews 4:15

We know that Jesus forgave those that crucified Him for while He was hanging on the cross, He cried out for their forgiveness. We also know that Jesus went out of His way to restore Peter after the resurrection because John gives us the details of the process in John 21. Jesus asks Peter three times if he loves Him, and we know Peter finally says, "Lord you know everything, you know I do."

Jesus knows our pain because He suffered pain. Jesus knows what it is like to be tempted with anger, bitterness, and revenge, for He must have been in order to relate to us in our struggles as the writer of Hebrews shared with us. Jesus knows.

Jesus walked in forgiveness and so must we. Jesus forgave when those that hurt Him didn't deserve it or earn it and so must we. Jesus forgave others without them even asking for it and so must we.

Let me be perfectly clear, this is not easy but it is required. Please carefully consider the following passages on the topic of forgiveness. If you read them slowly, prayerfully, and begin to understand the ramifications, they should send a shiver up our spines if we consider them deeply:

> Give us this day our daily bread, and forgive us our debts, as we also have forgiven our debtors. And lead us not into temptation but deliver us from evil. For if you forgive others their trespasses, your heavenly Father will also forgive you, but if you do not forgive others their trespasses, neither will your Father forgive your trespasses.
> Matthew 6:11-14

Do we really believe this passage? Jesus, while instructing His disciples in prayer, ties together provision, temptation *and* our Father's forgiveness to how we forgive those that have hurt, wounded, betrayed, or caused us pain.

Words like, "if" and "neither" should give us pause in this area of forgiveness. Yes, I know we are forgiven based on the blood of Jesus, yet, this passage nags at my mind and heart.

As does the story in Matthew 18. Most of us are familiar with the chapter and I mentioned it earlier. Church discipline is often the focus that we see in this chapter, but Matthew chose elsewhere how to end the chapter.

The Parable of the Unforgiving Servant completes the chapter and it has a chilling ending:

> So also, my heavenly Father will do to every one of you if you do not forgive your brother from your heart. Matthew 18:35

Do we believe this passage and what it implies? We know the story and are often upset with the wicked servant that refused to forgive someone that owed him a much smaller debt that he had just been forgiven, but do we make the application intended by Jesus?

"If we do not forgive our brother" should give us pause. Will God actually do the same thing to us if we fail to forgive? The passage certainly seems to say so. I am not proposing some new theology, simply urging that we elevate the importance of forgiveness that Jesus clearly states in this parable.

And whenever you stand praying, forgive, if you
have anything against anyone, so that your Father
also who is in heaven may forgive you your
trespasses. Mark 11:25

Have you ever been praying and God brings into your mind
a face from your past? Perhaps you keep reliving a painful
experience. Jesus instructs His disciples that when you are
praying and you realize that you need to forgive someone,
do so. Immediately. Why? "So that your Father in heaven
may forgive you!" Are the two aspects of forgiveness really
that connected in God's mind and ways? It would seem so.

I must let go in order to receive. It is difficult to receive
something when my hands are closed? If I hold on to anger,
hurt, bitterness, and my rights, it is hard to open my hands
and heart to my loving, Heavenly Father's gifts of grace,
mercy, forgiveness, and freedom. I can only hold so much
at any time.

Judge not, and you will not be judged; condemn not,
and you will not be condemned; forgive, and you will
be forgiven; Luke 6:37

We love the first part of this verse and even most
unbelievers can quote it – judge not! However, the verse
does not stop there. Forgiveness is also brought into the
company of judging and condemning. Ouch. Does this mean
that if we don't forgive others, we won't be forgiven? Why
would we take the chance? Forgive quickly as we have been
forgiven.

> Put on then, as God's chosen ones, holy and beloved, compassionate hearts, kindness, humility, meekness, and patience, bearing with one another and, if one has a complaint against another, forgiving each other; as the Lord has forgiven you, so you also must forgive. And above all these put on love, which binds everything together in perfect harmony.
> Colossians 3:12-14

Paul states clearly that if we have a complaint against anyone (and who does not?), we must forgive. How can we? Because the Lord has forgiven us, we must forgive.

What about those that hate us?

> "If you love those who love you, what benefit is that to you? For even sinners love those who love them. And if you do good to those who do good to you, what benefit is that to you? For even sinners do the same. And if you lend to those from whom you expect to receive, what credit is that to you? Even sinners lend to sinners, to get back the same amount. But love your enemies, and do good, and lend, expecting nothing in return, and your reward will be great, and you will be sons of the Most High, for he is kind to the ungrateful and the evil. Be merciful, even as your Father is merciful. Luke 6:32-36

There are other verses but these are sufficient to at least make us consider the benefits and problems centering around forgiveness.

If we hope to grow to where we can love those that hurt as we must begin with forgiveness. We must learn to release others from our pain.

Some of us remember the old cameras that took a picture that then came out of the front of the device. The picture would take a few minutes to become clear and we would marvel at the technology.

When someone hurts us deeply the temptation is to lock them into a snapshot photo. We take their face and freeze-frame it in the worst possible fashion and place it a deep place in our heart.

Every so often we take the photo out of our hearts and scream at it, maybe curse it, and speak all manner of evil against it. We relive the pain, hurt, words, and experience over and over again. In short, we have not forgiven the person that violated us. This is natural but certainly not godly.

If we are to freely receive God's forgiveness for our huge debt of sin, we must release those that hurt us from this dungeon of bitterness we keep them in. We have grown and changed over the years, and perhaps the culprit has as well. Even if they have not, we have been freely forgiven and according to all those verses we just read, we must forgive. We have no choice.

If we refuse, our destination is one of bitterness and guilt. The writer of Hebrews is clear:

> See to it that no one fails to obtain the grace of God;
> that no "root of bitterness" springs up and causes
> trouble, and by it many become defiled;
> Hebrews 12:15

Bitterness does not help anyone, and it certainly does not hurt the one that wounded us. In fact, they are rarely aware of our bitterness towards them. The old saying goes something like, "we drink poison thinking we are hurting the other person." How foolish.

One way to avoid becoming bitter is to move quickly to forgiveness. Release people to the hand of the Lord. God is more than capable of protecting your reputation, seeing that the guilty are punished, and of bringing about justice. We must forgive so we can be forgiven.

In another chapter, we will visit how to continue to relate with those that have deeply hurt us, for forgiving someone does not necessarily mean we become best friends or even friends at all. For now, let's take a few minutes and prayerfully consider the following questions.

For Our Consideration:

1. If the Lord can do anything, and He can, why does He allow for pain to enter into our lives?

2. Do you think it was easy for Jesus to forgive Judas and those that hurt Him?

3. Why does bitterness hurt others instead of just the one embracing it?

4. Why is forgiveness such a big deal to God?

5. Is there anyone that you need to forgive? Will you do so? If not, why not?

1 Corinthians 13:1-8 (a) (MSG)

If I speak with human eloquence and angelic ecstasy but don't love, I'm nothing but the creaking of a rusty gate.

If I speak God's Word with power, revealing all his mysteries and making everything plain as day, and if I have faith that says to a mountain, "Jump," and it jumps, but I don't love, I'm nothing.

If I give everything I own to the poor and even go to the stake to be burned as a martyr, but I don't love, I've gotten nowhere. So, no matter what I say, what I believe, and what I do, I'm bankrupt without love.

Love never gives up.
Love cares more for others than for self.
Love doesn't want what it doesn't have.
Love doesn't strut,
Doesn't have a swelled head,
Doesn't force itself on others,
Isn't always "me first,"
Doesn't fly off the handle,
Doesn't keep score of the sins of others,
Doesn't revel when others grovel,
Takes pleasure in the flowering of truth,
Puts up with anything,
Trusts God always,
Always looks for the best,
Never looks back,
But keeps going to the end. Love never dies.

~~~~~~

But not only is the exercise of Christian love a testimony unto the world of our Christian discipleship and a sure evidence of our own regeneration, but it is also that which delights God Himself.
Arthur W. Pink (1886-1952)

8. Loving the Unlovely

God chose what is low and despised in the world, even things that are not, to bring to nothing things that are, 1 Corinthians 1:28

Have you met someone and instantly didn't like them? I know, we are not supposed to do that as Christians, but if the truth is told, there are people that are hard to love.

Maybe they look strange, smell bad, perhaps they have an odd personality, or maybe they are so used to being rejected, it is easy to join in with everyone else.

Some are rude. Others completely inappropriate. Many are embarrassing to be around. Is there someone in your life that matches this description? Are you that someone to others?

Most of us are probably somewhere between wonderful and rejected. Handsome and ugly. Well-liked, sought out after socially and avoided. Most of us are normal.

Normal, of course, is one of those terms that the meaning of the word depends on who is using it. If you are old enough to remember the original Star Wars movie, there was a bar scene on a faraway planet where Luke is confronted by some strange being telling him that he looks weird! The creature telling Luke he looks funny is the point of the sarcasm in the scene, but I wonder how many of us feel like Luke? Perhaps we see ourselves like the other creature? Do we fit in or stand out?

Beauty is in the eye of the beholder, but it is probable that many of us struggle with being loved or loving others. Maybe it is physical, perhaps emotional, probably personality oriented, and definitely spiritual.

We have an enemy of our souls that hates us. This liar lies. Always. Jesus referred to him as the father of lies in John 8:44, and he is excellent in his craft. We must learn to know truth in order to defeat lies. A simple sentence that often takes a lifetime of growth to accomplish. This is especially true relationally speaking.

When we meet someone that is easy to reject we have a choice. What will we do? How will we treat them? How should we react and interact with this person?

There was a movement a few years back that though over commercialized, was true at its core. Tee-Shirts, bracelets, bumper stickers and all manner of paraphernalia was sold with WWJD written all over them.

"What Would Jesus Do?" is an excellent thought and important question.

We really don't have to read too far into the Gospel stories to find Jesus interacting with people outside of the acceptable. Jesus ate with sinners. Jesus hung out with the despised. Jesus touched the untouchables.

The inner circle of Jesus is telling. Zealots, a tax collector, and fishermen. Some women that followed Jesus around were those delivered from demons, prostitution, and all manner of evil. Jesus loved the unlovely.

Jesus was able to look past the social stigma, the rejection of others and see the hand of His Father in these men and women.

Matthew is one such person that received a special touch from Jesus. We tend to overlook the smallest details when it comes to this writer of the Gospel. Matthew did not.

> As Jesus passed on from there, he saw a man called Matthew sitting at the tax booth, and he said to him, "Follow me." And he rose and followed him.
> Matthew 9:9

We are familiar with this passage and the calling of one of Jesus' disciples. However, compare this verse to the other Gospel writer's account and see if you notice the difference.

> And as he passed by, he saw Levi the son of Alphaeus sitting at the tax booth, and he said to him, "Follow me." And he rose and followed him. Mark 2:14

> After this he went out and saw a tax collector named
> Levi, sitting at the tax booth. And he said to him,
> "Follow me." Luke 5:27

Matthew's calling is not recorded in John's Gospel, but did you see the difference between Matthew's account and the other two? No, I'm not referring to Levi vs. Matthew as far as his name. Look deeper.

You probably have heard how hated the tax collectors were by their fellow Israelites. Most were corrupt men that made their living by cheating their friends and relatives. Despised is a bit too kind of a word for these men.

Did you find the difference in the way Matthew wrote it? Matthew includes the word "man" in his account. Jesus saw a man, not simply a tax collector. Not a villain. Not a worthless cheat. Not a loser, but a man. Matthew, for the first time in many years, felt like a man because this Man called his name. Matthew dropped everything and followed Jesus and never forgot that look in Jesus' eye.

We probably remember another tax collector as well named Zacchaeus. Jesus violated every respectable custom and went into the man's home. In fact, Jesus told this little man up in a tree, "I must stay at your house today." In that same section of the story, Jesus declares that Zacchaeus is also a son of Abraham, and that would have been a shock to most people.

Did you know that the very first time Jesus shared the fact that He was the Messiah was with the woman at the well in John 4? Why her? Why then? Of all the places and all of the people to choose, why her? Jesus loved the unlovely. Five husbands and the man you are now living with is not your husband! How would we respond to her? Jesus gave her living water and a revelation.

Beyond Jesus' disciples and those He ate with, He did the unthinkable. You probably can't relate to the following unless you have actually been around lepers.

> And Jesus stretched out his hand and touched him, saying, "I will; be clean." And immediately his leprosy was cleansed. Matthew 8:3

Lepers were the lowest of the lowest in the social order. Despised, rejected, outcasts, lonely, commanded by the Law to cover themselves and shout out "unclean, unclean" whenever they were near another human. Unlovely does not begin to describe this group of people.

Having spent a brief time among some lepers in China, I received a glimpse of what these Biblical characters must have lived like. Sadly, the lepers I visited were probably better off than the ones in the Scriptures.

Did you notice what Jesus did to the most unlovely person possible? The man that had lived without any human touch for a very long time was touched by Love Himself. Jesus simply could have spoken the word of healing, but in this case, He touched the untouchable.

I am sure there was a gasp from the crowd and Jesus's disciples as He did the unthinkable and touched this man. Most people would carry rocks or quickly find one and hurl it at any leper that dared to come close. Jesus touched him, and my cold, hard heart is challenged to its core.

The Bible is a story of redemption from cover to cover. God chooses the foolish, debased, despised, unexpected and rejected to further His work and Kingdom. He always has.

fffffffffff

David was the youngest son of eight. Who was Solomon's mother again? Joseph was a hated brother and a slave. So were Daniel and his three friends. The heroes of faith in Hebrews chapter 11 looks more like a list of misfits and social rejects than people we would want to be friends with, yet in God's eyes, they were His beloved creation.

Paul's words ring true:

> For the foolishness of God is wiser than men, and the weakness of God is stronger than men. For consider your calling, brothers: not many of you were wise according to worldly standards, not many were powerful, not many were of noble birth. But God chose what is foolish in the world to shame the wise; God chose what is weak in the world to shame the strong; 1 Corinthians 1:25-27

I'm in that list and so are you. Most of us are not of noble birth and many times feel weak and foolish. Yet, Jesus touched us! Jesus gives us worth, value, and purpose, not because we are lovely but because He loves us and makes us worthy.

How do we love the unlovely? We begin to see others through the eyes of our Savior. We study how Jesus interacted with the unlovely of His day and we imitate Him. We pray for a new heart of love to embrace those that need one so desperately.

Jesus looked past the outside and saw His Father's hand of creation in each person. Can we? Will we? Can we choose to do acts of kindness even for those that irritate us? Of course, we can, but will we choose to do so?

We did not deserve God's mercy, grace and the richness of His love and neither does anyone else. Jesus loved us and therefore we must learn to love others.

Jesus saw men in Matthew and Zacchaeus, not simply the evil they were engaged in. Jesus saw a hurting woman at the well and not just an immoral sinner. Jesus looked past the filth, rejection, and pain of a social outcast leper and met a need far deeper than physical healing, He touched his soul.

We have the opportunity to be the hands of Jesus in our day. We have Matthew's and lepers and outcasts all around us that need a touch of the Master's hand. Will we reach out to them in His name and through His love?

If you are the leper, woman at the well or tax collector, there is hope in Jesus. All of us are less than we can and should be. All of us have sinned, fallen short, and failed numerous times. The only perfect person was Jesus. All the rest of us are in varying degrees of imperfection.

Don't believe the lies of the enemy of our souls that you are too far gone, too unlovely, too forsaken to be loved. Jesus died for you and He lives now to make you into a brand-new creation in Him. He loves you.

If you have areas of your life you need to change, and we all do, then go to our loving heavenly Father through the name of Jesus Christ and find forgiveness and healing. If you ask, you will receive.

After you receive salvation, forgiveness, or a new purpose in life, don't keep the good news to yourself. Find someone else to reach out to and share the good news of salvation and acceptance.

There are unlovely, hurting people all around us. Look around. Reach out. Share the love. Watch the unlovely change into beauty by the love of the Savior. He did it for me and He can and will do it for you if you ask Him. You can be restored, renewed and reborn in Christ!

For Our Consideration:

1. Is there someone in our life that just drives you crazy? Why do they? What do you think is behind the irritation?

2. Does love need an outlet? Why or why not?

3. Is it really possible for us to imitate Jesus? Why or why not?

4. How can we grow in our love of those that are unlovely?

5. Are we willing to reach out to others and take a risk with love? Why or why not?

1 Corinthians 13:1-8 (a) (NKJV)

Though I speak with the tongues of men and of angels but have not love, I have become sounding brass or a clanging cymbal.

And though I have the gift of prophecy, and understand all mysteries and all knowledge, and though I have all faith, so that I could remove mountains, but have not love, I am nothing.

And though I bestow all my goods to feed the poor, and though I give my body to be burned, but have not love, it profits me nothing.

Love suffers long and is kind; love does not envy; love does not parade itself, is not puffed up; does not behave rudely, does not seek its own, is not provoked, thinks no evil; does not rejoice in iniquity, but rejoices in the truth; bears all things, believes all things, hopes all things, endures all things.

Love never fails.

~~~~~~

How can one who loves the Lord Jesus in sincerity choose but to love all saints, though of different persuasions, since, notwithstanding that difference, they all are so dear to Him that He gave His life as a ransom for them all?
Nathaniel Vincent (1638-1697)

91

9. Saying No And Walking Away Can Be Love

Never trust your tongue when your heart is bitter –
Anonymous

Tough love has been embraced and encouraged, argued over and dismissed by many. We need to give grace vs. we need to be strong for their own good. I'm not sure I see these as two opposites, but many do. I'm all for grace and I am also all for personal responsibility. Discipline and mercy. We need more of all of the above and not less.

Throughout this book, I have tried to explain love in terms of action while not dismissing the emotional side of it. We are emotional creatures and we must learn to embrace these gifts while not being controlled by them. God gave us both emotions and a mind, feelings, and thinking. They should complement each other not dominate or exclude one another. We need both.

What do we do when we have tried everything to love someone and they refuse to change? While there are never simple answers, there are choices we can make.

For example, we need not stay in an abusive situation just to show love to someone. Unless we are being persecuted for our faith in Jesus, I don't find any verses in the Scripture that endorse abuse. Or the submitting to it. If you are living with someone that is abusing you, leave, and do it now.

If that person is your spouse, I am not necessarily advocating divorce, but you do not have to stay in that situation. Seek counsel and get help. Now. Today.

If that person is a family member and you are being abused, tell someone today. Now. Right now. You are not showing love to that person by submitting to abuse. In fact, you are hurting them and not loving them. Sin loves the dark and hates being exposed.

By your silence and acceptance of their behavior, you are reinforcing the rightness of the deeds in their mind. That is not helpful or loving, and that is encouraging them to continue on with their sinful behavior. The most loving thing you could possibly do is expose it, not live with it or cover it over.

Saying no can be an act of love. For example, what about enabling a free-loader in your home? Or, providing funds for someone to continue on with a drinking or drug problem? Are we really helping them by saying yes? Would it be more loving to refuse their request or to continue to aid them in sin and failure?

One time a friend came to me and asked me for some money to get them out of a jam. It just happened that I had some extra cash, so I gave it to him. Later, as I was musing and praying, I believe the Lord stated clearly to me that I had interfered in His plan. The rebuke went something like, "I had him right where I wanted him and you helped him escape. You never even asked Me if you should give the money and now this brother will have to go through another set of circumstances to accomplish My will for him."

I learned that day that I could do something that was good but not right. My heart was in the right place, but I didn't have all of the information necessary to make the correct choice. We rarely do.

By bailing out my friend I did not help him. I did not display love, though my actions were prompted by love. I should have asked the Lord how He wanted me to spend His money before I gave it away.

What about panhandlers and those asking for money? Aren't we supposed to give to those that ask of us? Yes, but wisdom is in order. If someone needs food, buy them a meal. If they need gasoline for their car, pump it for them. Just giving them cash often does more harm than good. Not always, but we must learn to ask the Lord first. Sometimes saying no is the right answer. The loving answer.

How many loving parents tell their children no when they are asking for something that will harm them? Would saying yes be the best when saying no is clearly the right choice?

Many times, parents interfere in a child's eating, recreational choices, friendships, and a host of other items and say no. Letting a child do damage to themselves or to others is not love. We help restrain them until they are old enough to make better choices. This is love.

We must learn to see the cause and effect of our choices. Enabling abuse or neglect is not love. Some parents have helped cripple their adult children by trying to love them through over-protection and over-provision.

We all know the story of the caterpillar struggling to get free from the cocoon and what happens if we assist it. We want to ease the struggle but end up hurting the butterfly by doing so. It is hard to watch our children struggle but struggle they must if they are to learn to fly.

Divorce:

Sometimes relationships are toxic and must be ended. To do so is love, though often not recognized. Destroying each other is not love and ending the relationship can be the highest form of true love. It may be a kindness to walk away while staying would simply be destructive.

I am in no way justifying divorce or walking out on personal responsibility; I'm saying that in some cases leaving is better than staying for all involved. Divorce is a cancer and the children are often the victims of parents ignoring Biblical love.

Divorce should be the last option, not the first choice. However, divorce is not the unpardonable sin, and God certainly allowed for divorce in both Testaments. As shocking as it may be, even God used the term to describe His putting away of Israel:

Thus says the Lord: "Where is your mother's certificate of divorce, with which I sent her away? Or which of my creditors is it to whom I have sold you? Behold, for your iniquities you were sold, and for your transgressions, your mother was sent away. Isaiah 50:1

She saw that for all the adulteries of that faithless one, Israel, I had sent her away with a decree of divorce. Yet her treacherous sister Judah did not fear, but she too went and played the whore. Jeremiah 3:8

Redemption and reconciliation is, of course, the first order of business, but if impossible, God allows for leaving. Many argue over whether the divorce is the sin or the remarrying and I will not settle the issue here, nor do I wish to fight about it. My main point is that sometimes it is in the best interest of everyone involved for the marriage to end, and divorce is not something that people should be considered as second-class Christians if they have walked through it.

While many use divorce as a quick escape hatch to difficult problems, that is not what I am endorsing. God values marriage and it is the highest form of commitment we can make outside of salvation. We must not destroy our marriages for the sake of pleasure, sin or immorality and then excuse the divorce or use it as an escape hatch.

Difficulties in marriage are normal and this covenant relationship provides excellent opportunities for true,

Biblical love to flourish. Marriage is not to be entered lightly or exited easily.

If a marriage must be ended it is a loss, not a gain and a defeat, not a victory. Sometimes we all have defeats, but please don't take what I have written as an excuse for, or justification of divorce. Every divorce for any reason is a shame and if children are involved, destructive.

With that being said, there are still times when divorce is acceptable and better than staying in the relationship. Please seek godly counsel from qualified leaders before jumping in or out of a marriage.

Destructive Relationships:

The Scriptures are clear regarding who and how we pick friends:

> Whoever walks with the wise becomes wise, but the companion of fools will suffer harm. Proverbs 13:20

> The one who keeps the law is a son with understanding, but a companion of gluttons shames his father. Proverbs 28:7

> He who loves wisdom makes his father glad, but a companion of prostitutes squanders his wealth. Proverbs 29:3

"You win or lose by the friends you choose," was a sentence from a children's song we used to quote quite a bit when our children were young. It is a true thought. Friends will lead us somewhere and we need to wise about the destination.

Most of us probably had friends when we were growing up the helped us act more mature. We probably also had that one friend that we simply couldn't be around all that much because we slipped into sinful behavior.

There are some relationships that drive us towards carnality, sinful thoughts and behaviors. Is it loving to remain in those friendships or is it more loving to limit them? I guess the answer depends on where you want to end up. If we want to walk in a manner worthy of our Lord, then choosing to walk away from a destructive relationship is love.

Some friends encourage us and others destroy us. Some challenge us to step up and others dare us to sin and push moral boundaries. Some relationships are meant to be long term and others are a danger to be avoided. Love will choose properly.

There are some relationships that lead to life and others that lead to sin and death. If we are going to walk in a manner that is pleasing to the Lord, we will choose life and avoid sin and death.

I am very grateful to my wife and daughters that have pointed out dangerous relationships to me over the last forty years of ministry. Pastors are sometimes the targets of the opposite sex that want to entrap them in immorality.

The women in my life have warned me to stay away from certain people, or at least to be very careful around them. This is not an insult, but a protection. Paul said we are to flee immorality:

> Flee from sexual immorality. Every other sin a person commits is outside the body, but the sexually immoral person sins against his own body.
> 1 Corinthians 6:18

Sometimes we are told to stand and fight and, in this case, we are told to run away! There are times when saying no to a relationship is wiser than saying yes.

There are times when we must leave a church, change jobs, and move out of a neighborhood. These changes can be based in love and leaving does not mean it is a defeat.

There are seasons and they do change and come to an end. Love can be leaving instead of staying and making relationships difficult.

There is a time to act in love and leave a church if our presence causes conflict and division. The same can be true for ministry groups, mission organizations, and even sports teams.

Sometimes the best thing we can do is leave. I am not saying that leaving always the best answer, but it certainly can be at times. We must seek the Lord and hear His voice in each case.

Love isn't always easy and sometimes is very painful. Choosing to think of others over ourselves can be emotionally hurtful. But, we must walk in love. We must learn to think of others and what is best for them even if it costs us personally. Sometimes that hurts, deeply.

Love sometimes says no, and sometimes love demands that we remove ourselves from the relationship or situation. Love does not seek its own way but choices are made that are best for others.

Love is not always pretty and sometimes can be very messy. Since love, Biblical love, is a choice, choosing against our own interests sometimes hurts very much. But, we must choose love. Always. Even when it hurts.

Jesus said we lay down our lives to show great love, and dying to ourselves is rarely fun, but it always is the best choice. If we die to ourselves we will embrace life through Christ, and that is always is the best decision to make.

For Our Consideration:

1. Can you think of any personal examples where saying no was acting in love?

2. Is there ever a time when marriages should end? Why or why not?

3. Is there ever a time to leave a church or friendship, job or location? Explain.

4. What does dying to yourself mean to you? Give an example.

1 Corinthians 13:1-8 (a) (AMP)

If I speak with the tongues of men and of angels but have not love [for others growing out of God's love for me], then I have become only a noisy gong or a clanging cymbal [just an annoying distraction].

And if I have the gift of prophecy [and speak a new message from God to the people], and understand all mysteries, and [possess] all knowledge; and if I have all [sufficient] faith so that I can remove mountains, but do not have love [reaching out to others], I am nothing.

If I give all my possessions to feed the poor, and if I surrender my body to be burned, but do not have love, it does me no good at all.

Love endures with patience and serenity, love is kind and thoughtful, and is not jealous or envious; love does not brag and is not proud or arrogant.

It is not rude; it is not self-seeking, it is not provoked [nor overly sensitive and easily angered]; it does not take into account a wrong endured.
It does not rejoice at injustice but rejoices with the truth [when right and truth prevail].

Love bears all things [regardless of what comes], believes all things [looking for the best in each one], hopes all things [remaining steadfast during difficult times], endures all things [without weakening].

Love never fails [it never fades nor ends]

~~~~~~

Love is the vital spirits of a Christian, which are the principles of all motion and lively operation. Where there is a failure in these, the soul is in decay. Hugh Binning (1627-1653)

10. Love Will Change the World

As one person I cannot change the world, but I can change the world of one person. – Paul Shane Spear

This world is fading away and will be replaced with a Kingdom of love ruled by Love Himself. Until that day we still live in a fallen world dominated by something other than love.

Each of us can do something for someone else to help make their world a bit better. We cannot do everything that needs to be done but that should not stop us from doing something. Sadly, it often does.

We all want to make a big difference in this life. We want to do the grand things that will make us easy to remember for generations.

The truth is that those huge events often take place in the realm of the normal. I don't recall any Scripture mentioning receiving a reward for doing the big, exceptional, exciting, earth-moving things. I do recall these:

> One who is faithful in a very little is also faithful in much, and one who is dishonest in a very little is also dishonest in much. Luke 16:10

> Moreover, it is required of stewards that they be found faithful. 1 Corinthians 4:2

> But the fruit of the Spirit is love, joy, peace, patience, kindness, goodness, faithfulness, Galatians 5:22

God wants His children to be faithful in doing what they are called to do. God may grant a huge following or give you a wildly successful business or ministry. He may not.

God may want you to serve in a manner that is not seen by men. God may want us to do in secret what He rewards in public:

> But when you pray, go into your room and shut the door and pray to your Father who is in secret. And your Father who sees in secret will reward you. Matthew 6:6

The truth is we do not have enough information to know whether what we are doing is really important in God's economy. Maybe the actions that are applauded by an earthly realm are not all that valuable in a heavenly one.

Heaven seems to function on a different value system than earth. The streets are paved with gold there, while we use asphalt or concrete here. If you want to be great in that Kingdom you must become a servant, while down here, we attempt to climb over everyone else to rise in status.

I wonder what would happen if we really did attempt to do what Jesus clearly said to do? Would our world be different if we chose obedience instead of excuse making? Consider these passages for just a moment:

> Do nothing from selfish ambition or conceit but in humility count others more significant than yourselves. Philippians 2:3

Does the Word of God really mean nothing here? What would happen in our homes, churches, places of employment, shopping and even driving, if we really did count others more significant than ourselves? If we really did put others first and esteem them, would our lives change?

> By this, we know love, that he laid down his life for us, and we ought to lay down our lives for the brothers. 1 John 3:16

We all know John 3:16, but what would happen in our daily world if we put this thought from 1 John in practice? What if we really did lay down our lives for others? What if we gave them the first place, the best, and the honor? Are we willing to look in the mirror and ask if we really are laying down our lives for everyone else?

> Look carefully then how you walk, not as unwise but as wise, making the best use of the time because the days are evil. Therefore, do not be foolish, but understand what the will of the Lord is. And do not get drunk with wine, for that is debauchery, but be filled with the Spirit, addressing one another in psalms and hymns and spiritual songs, singing and making melody to the Lord with your heart, giving thanks always and for everything to God the Father in the name of our Lord Jesus Christ, submitting to one another out of reverence for Christ.
> Ephesians 5:15-21

Paul states a great deal in this short section. We are to be careful how we live our lives and not to be foolish in doing so. Don't waste our time getting drunk but grow in understanding what our Lord wants from us.

At least part of what the Lord wants is for us to be filled with the Spirit and sing, to always give thanks, and learn how to submit one to another in love!

What would happen if we really did do that? What would our marriage look like if we focused on the Scriptures and attempted to always give thanks for everything?

What would change if we really did attempt to submit to others instead of insisting that we get our own way? I wonder if our hearts would soften and our words would change? Perhaps even those we are around would notice.

> Let no corrupting talk come out of your mouths, but
> only such as is good for building up, as fits the
> occasion, that it may give grace to those who hear.
> Ephesians 4:29

Life and death are in the power of the tongue, Solomon
said in Proverbs 18:21, but do we really believe it? What if
our conversations changed to giving grace instead of
tearing up one another? What place would gossip, slander,
malice, or anger have in our lives?

What if we really did attempt to filter our words, would
our relationships be better or worse for the effort? What if
our goal was to dispense grace to others instead of
something, anything so far less? Remember God does say
this in His Word:

> But he gives more grace. Therefore, it says, "God
> opposes the proud but gives grace to the humble."
> James 4:6

> Likewise, you who are younger, be subject to the
> elders. Clothe yourselves, all of you, with humility
> toward one another, for "God opposes the proud but
> gives grace to the humble." 1 Peter 5:5

How do we get more grace in our lives and
relationships? Perhaps the answer is in these verses.
Humble ourselves and resist self-pride and focus in all
areas. What would happen if we really did attempt these
goals?

If the Church of Jesus Christ really did attempt to imitate our Lord by laying down our lives one for another, we would begin to change the world.

We can't change everything but each of us can change something and we must. The Church should be known for love, grace, mercy, service, and kindness. Giving should be the norm and financial or sexual fraud should be unheard of within our midst.

We should be known as a gathering of people that are warm, welcoming, and loving. What would happen in our world if we really did these things?

As we walk through 1 Corinthians 13 one last time together, ask yourself what needs to be changed in you and your relationships. I can be overwhelmed when I see all of the problems in the world and the Church, but Jesus didn't ask me to correct or to be responsible for everything, only those things in my realm of influence.

We can change our world by making choices. We can be an influence and make a difference that lasts for generations and we can begin today. The real question is, will we?

1 Corinthians 13:4-8(a):

Love is patient and kind – Will I pray daily that the Lord would grant me the ability to be patient and kind with everyone in my life, beginning with those in my home? As I learn to practice these choices in the home, will I ask the Lord to extend these behaviors to others outside of my family? Church? Work? School? Shopping? Playing?

Love does not envy or boast – Will I choose to be thankful for what I see God doing in the lives of others? When someone is blessed or praised, will I rejoice with them? Will I not turn the focus on me and my life constantly, but focus on others instead? Will I embrace humility instead of self-focus? Will I lay down personal competition and learn to actually listen to others?

It is not arrogant or rude – Will I make a decision to guard my words and weigh them before speaking to make sure they produce life in the hearer and not death? Rude is sometimes translated to act unbecomingly. Will I choose to act in a way that is honorable and others-focused? Will I actively listen to others without interrupting them to get my two cents in?

It does not insist on its own way – Will I seek to take up the Cross of Jesus daily and learn to appreciate the viewpoints of others? Will I allow others to think and act differently without judgment upon them? Will I set others free from having to think and act just as I do? Will I allow God the Holy Spirit to do His work and not attempt to take His place in the life of others?

It is not irritable or resentful – Will I learn to overlook an offense? Can I allow others to think and act differently than I do without being upset, jealous, or pouty? If someone receives praise can I rejoice with them and not become envious of their position? Will I allow others to enjoy their life without being irritable over their freedom in Christ?

It does not rejoice at wrongdoing – Will I resist enjoying seeing those that I don't like suffer or being taken down a peg or two? Will I not enjoy the off-color humor or wickedness all around me? Will I learn to grieve over what breaks God's heart? Will I attempt to defend the weak and stand up for those that cannot?

But rejoices with the truth – Will I always attempt to walk in truth, not lies? Will I accept what is right even when it is harmful to my self-interests? Will I learn to speak the truth in love?

Love bears all things – Will I make a choice to put up with others? Will I learn to cheerfully accept whatever God brings into my life for His glory? Will I learn to quit complaining and begin rejoicing instead? Will I rejoice in God's sovereignty, especially in my life?

Believes all things – Will I accept the Word of God as true? Will I believe the best of others instead of the worst? Will I give grace to others like I want them to give grace to me? Will I not assign bad motives to others while demanding to receive grace for my own?

Hopes all things – Hope typically means the earnest expectation of good, so will I be a person of faith and not doubt? Will I expect God to redeem and work out everything for His good pleasure? Will I choose to excel in good, not evil? Will I expand my view to the eternal and not simply the temporal?

Endures all things – Will I learn to rejoice always and pray without ceasing? Will I learn to limit my words to those that bring life and not death? Will I not run but stand fast upon God's Word and His promises? Will I learn to swear to my own hurt instead of seeking the easy way out? Will I be faithful until the end?

We know that Paul goes on to state that love never ends. How could it since God is love and He is eternal? The above exercise is simply an example of how we may take this familiar passage and prayerfully walk through it asking God to help us grow and mature in love.

As we close, I would ask you to prayerfully go through the definition of love again and ask the Lord to gently remind you of areas that you need to grow in. If you ask the Lord to change you, He will provide many opportunities for that change to occur. These situations will most likely involve people that you know, and there will be plenty of changes to get this right. After all, love can and will change the world as we learn to walk in it like Jesus did.

We did not cover everything surrounding love, for God is love and is beyond complete understanding. What I hope has occurred with this written effort is that we would be drawn to our Lord and Savior and that this would produce more love for others.

In fact, my prayer is that if we would know Love Himself deeply, then we would be more willing to choose to walk in His footsteps and perhaps, even the world would know we are His disciples.

For Our Consideration:

1. What does God is love mean to you after reading this book?

2. As you read through the book, was there anything that specifically stood out to you that perhaps you hadn't thought before?

3. Are there any people that God has brought to your mind that you need to work on loving more?

4. Do you believe that Biblical love is what God is after for His children? Why or why not?

~~~~~~

There is no greater way to win one another's love as by denying ourselves to seek one another's wealth.
Ralph Venning (1622-1674)

11. Love Lifted Me

My Story of Meeting Love Himself

Growing up in a home that was populated with mostly anger, constant arguing, sexual abuse and selfishness, love was rarely seen. Oh, there was lust, profanity, sexual perversion and the pursuit of pleasure, but not love. At least, not God's love.

We maintained an outward appearance of religion, being infrequent participants in the Roman Catholic faith, but the only time Jesus' name was uttered violated multiple commandments.

Both of my parents professed a relationship with Jesus eventually, and for that I am grateful. My mother has passed on to her reward, and my father lives close to us and is nearly ninety.

My parents did the best they knew how to do so this retelling of my life story is not meant as a slam on them. I am not sure they were ever fully aware of how their relationship and my brother's treatment of me impacted my life.

My dad was in an accident in a papermill factory when I was just a young boy, and the doctors discovered cancer in his leg. Multiple surgeries later a metal pipe was inserted into the leg after removing the knee. Being told he would never walk again, this accident left us in deep need and added great stress to an already overstressed family.

My mother went to work in a department store for several years to provide income for the family. This was a type of love in action and without it, we would have lost everything. In those days there were no programs in place to assist injured workers.

My mother was a rather loud, boisterous, bitter woman that verbally badgered my father day and night. She was deeply hurt, and she only knew one outlet for that wound.

The good aspect of this particular skill was that she goaded my father, through questioning his manhood, into walking. After being told by the doctors that he would probably never walk again, my dad did get back up and even reentered the job force.

We moved to another city while I was in the fourth grade and then again in the seventh grade. The first move was from Erie, Pennsylvania to Little Rock, Arkansas, and it felt like a cross-culture experience.

In those days party telephone lines were still normal. If you don't know what those are, Google it. One day I remember picking up the phone and the minister's wife across the street was talking about those _____ Yankee

Catholics that moved in recently. Not exactly a warm welcome to the South. The time there in Arkansas was good for me and not so much for anyone else. I was running free outdoors most of the time and the more often I was out of the house the better.

Three years later we moved again, this time to the Kansas City area, and we settled in for good.

I was now in the seventh grade. My older brother by four years did not want to have a nerdy geek for a little brother so he introduced me to the world of drugs and alcohol consumption.

This began a journey that would take quite a toll on a young man not quite in his teens. Over the next few years, drugs were plentiful and so was sexual exploration.

These were the days of Woodstock and free love. Get high, go to bed with someone and live the dream. God was nowhere in my thinking or life and He was not missed. My only previous experience with Him was a dead religious service mostly in Latin and a hate-filled bigot on the phone. No thanks.

The world system had no answers for a young man destroying his life and there was a spiritual hole forming in my heart. There was also a physical one developing in my stomach. Eventually, the pain was so intense I was taken to the doctor. This would be in my Freshman year of high school.

I had developed an ulcer from all of the speed (amphetamines) taken and they were eating a hole in my stomach. After reviewing his findings, the doctor asked me if I wanted to tell my parents or if he should? I did and it was not pretty.

My oldest brother had moved out the day he graduated from high school and married a woman that my mother hated. My middle brother had been arrested while shooting out lights under the influence of LSD, and now I was wasting away through the usage of hard drugs. What were they going to do with me?

The answer, was, of course, to help me with counselling. The group they found was called DIG – Drug Intervention Group and met at, where else, but in a very liberal church.

Their answer to my hard drug problem was simple – smoke marijuana and quit destroying your stomach. That sounded good to me, so I hooked up with some guys and began to smoke pot every day and limited my LSD and hard drug usage to the weekends. The stomach problem was solved!

The hole in the heart was not. I eventually met a girl named Leslie. I was smitten from the first glance and decided that is was the one for me. I began to pursue her with every charm a long-haired, dirty, never washed his clothes, always stoned out of his mind guy had.

For reasons neither of us can explain, this Christian young lady agreed to go out with me. She should not have and she did pay a price for her compromise. However, God is gracious and He did eventually redeem the entire situation for His glory.

This girl would share with me regularly about her relationship with Jesus. She had a similar family history and drug background to mine so she was well aware of my stalling and avoidance tactics.

I told her I had my religion and didn't need anything else. One comforting fact about being a Catholic, no matter how wicked you are, you have a pretty good chance of just spending some time in purgatory and then getting out sooner or later. (A theological rebuttal to this error is beyond the goal of this testimony, but boy is it needed!)

One night in 1973 I was attending a concert high on LSD. Rather than hearing the concert though, all I could here was Leslie's preaching to me about Jesus. It ruined the whole evening. Or did it?

Something had been stirring in my soul through this time. There was an aching and there was a lack that no amount of sex, drugs, or booze could fill. Something else was missing.

On another occasion, my friends and I were sitting around smoking dope and an older guy (age 22) was in the back of a van parked nearby. I could hear him calling out, almost crying because he could no longer see the veins in his arms and he needed help to inject the drugs.

We had experimented with "hitting up" and so I knew what he was doing. As I sat there thinking with what was left of my mind, I began to compare the life this man had, and the one Leslie had shared about with me.

One ended up in a painful, meaningless death and one had the promise of not only an earthly life that mattered but an eternal one. Let's see, heaven vs. hell. Freedom from drugs vs. peace. Hmmm. It really was not much of a choice at that moment.

My heart was becoming tender to the offer of salvation and I was beginning to understand what I needed saving from.

The final push came in the form of a dream. I have had two supernatural dreams in my life and neither were pleasant. In this one, a tremendous fear came over me to the point where I was shaking. The entire world turned silver and there was this horrible demonic mocking voice that I couldn't drown out. Sweat poured out of me and I found myself begging God to help me. Then I awoke.

I had made my decision and it was not just an emotional one. The life I was living was not a life and the future was even worse. The offer of eternal life along with the forgiveness of my sins was starting to make sense to me. I decided that the next time Leslie invited me to church I would go forward and answer the call!

On July 25, 1973, we went to church. They were showing a movie entitled "Thief in the Night." I really don't remember much about the movie other than a girl screaming though most of it for missing the rapture, but I went forward afterwards and prayed for forgiveness of my sins.

I know now what happened far better than I knew then. Almost immediately peace came into a troubled life. The drugs and booze fell away and a love for the Scriptures was birthed in my heart. I was not perfect and still am not today, but I was a new creation on a new journey.

The King of Love came into my heart through the presence of the Holy Spirit. My sin was forgiven and I was born again. A new life was gained that day.

For the first time, I met Love. I knew what it meant to be born again. To leave the kingdom of darkness and to enter into the Kingdom of Love and Light.

The journey began that day and continues to this one. I am a new creation in Christ living each day with a purpose and I am now a citizen of a new Kingdom – the Kingdom of Love.

If you want to join me in this journey, if you have heard the sweet, still, small voice of Love calling to you, consider the following and pray for the Savior, Who is Love, to show you what Love is really all about. Here is what God has said in His Word and He cannot lie!

For I am not ashamed of the gospel, for it is the power of God for salvation to everyone who believes, to the Jew first and also to the Greek. Romans 1:16

Because, if you confess with your mouth that Jesus is Lord and believe in your heart that God raised him from the dead, you will be saved. For with the heart one believes and is justified, and with the mouth, one confesses and is saved. Romans 1:9-10

For "everyone who calls on the name of the Lord will be saved." Romans 10:13

Then he brought them out and said, "Sirs, what must I do to be saved?" And they said, "Believe in the Lord Jesus, and you will be saved, you and your household." Acts 16:30-31

This Jesus is the stone that was rejected by you, the builders, which has become the cornerstone. And there is salvation in no one else, for there is no other name under heaven given among men by which we must be saved. Acts 4:11-12

For God so loved the world, that he gave his only Son, that whoever believes in him should not perish but have eternal life. For God did not send his Son

into the world to condemn the world, but in order that the world might be saved through him.
 John 3:16-17

And you were dead in the trespasses and sins in which you once walked, following the course of this world, following the prince of the power of the air, the spirit that is now at work in the sons of disobedience— among whom we all once lived in the passions of our flesh, carrying out the desires of the body and the mind, and were by nature children of wrath, like the rest of mankind. But God, being rich in mercy, because of the great love with which he loved us, even when we were dead in our trespasses, made us alive together with Christ—by grace you have been saved— and raised us up with him and seated us with him in the heavenly places in Christ Jesus, so that in the coming ages he might show the immeasurable riches of his grace in kindness toward us in Christ Jesus.
For by grace you have been saved through faith. And this is not your own doing; it is the gift of God, not a result of works, so that no one may boast.
Ephesians 2:1-9

 These verses are simply a sampling of the heart of God and the way to find a new life in Christ. If you read these and decide that Jesus is indeed the answer, then pray something like this:

Father, I know I am a sinner who is lost, hurting and in desperate need of saving. I know I have failed in so many ways and I need Your forgiveness. I do believe that Jesus Christ is the Savior and that His blood was shed for my sins. Please save me, let me be born again, wash my sin and guilt away forever!

If you pray something like that prayer and trust your life into the Savior's hand, your life will never be the same! God will begin a new work in you that will change everything from now on.

If you did pray then go get a Bible and find others to share this excellent news with - and welcome to the Family!

Love Gems

Wisdom from some other friends on Love

What follows are some insights from others that know Love Himself. Enjoy the variety and depth of this wisdom and may the Lord enlarge your vision of Him.

Inclusion of thoughts does not necessarily imply full agreement with all doctrines of the authors...sounds like an insurance exclusion but added just in case you were wondering.

Love in Action

I heard a song by Stephen Stills.
He sang "Love the one you're with."
And now I see those words are true
because Love is God's great gift.
Love the ones who love the Lord.
Love strangers and the poor.
Show love by helping where they hurt.
Show love that Christ came for.
So, love your neighbor as yourself
then put your love in action.
And when you love your enemies
it gives your faith real traction.
It opens hearts that have grown cold
and softens the objections
that non-believers have, to God.
Love makes a real connection.
No one cares what you may know
until they know you care.
So, if you show God's Love and Grace,
they'll listen when you share.
And you can share that Jesus came
to pay the price of sin.
And only by accepting him
will eternal life begin.
If you show love to some pour soul
and do it in Christ's name
Then they may help someone they know
and witness to the claim
that all the world will see our faith
in the holy God above
and they'll know that we are Christians
by God's Grace and by our love.
©Jeff Hildebrandt · viewfromthepew@hotmail.com

Jeff Hildebrandt is a Christian Cowboy Poet who lives in Denver. His View-From-The-Pew poetry is heard regularly on the Salem Media radio stations, KRKS Am & FM.

Do You See Me Now?

Proverbs 21:13
Whoever shuts their ears to the cry of the poor will also cry out and not be answered.

Do you see me as I jump into your arms? Watch me laugh as I sprint across the courtyard!

Do you see me?

Do you see me as I swing? I can go so high! My dirty little feet can almost touch the sky!

Do you see me?

Do you see me as I slip on down the slide? It is fast and it is fun.

Do you see me?

Do you see me eat the candy? The taste is very fine. My grinning mouth is smeared with sugar.

Do you see me?

Do you see that courtyard? There is trash all over. Criss crosses from the rain cut through sand to reveal the muddy dirt.

Do you see it?

Do you see the swing? The chains are rough and rusted and only the sun-hot metal frame of the wooden seat remains.

Do you see it?

Do you know that the slide is cracked here and there and there? It cuts my arm a bit.

Do you see it?

Do you see my teeth? The candy and no toothbrush has rotted them away. I'm only 6 years old.

Do you see it?

Do you feel my arms around your neck? Do you see my smile? Do you see me hug you, and never let you go.

Do you see me?

Do you see the boy? His eyes reach out to you! Do you see his pain? The drugs, the fights, the poverty rips his family to shreds. He knows there is a better way. But he is so broken. Will you let the darkness in him stay?

Do you see him?

Do you see his older sister? Nearly dead was she. The drugs she took only to escape the life of pain and poverty. "There is no better home for me! There is no better life! I take the drugs to escape my parents' drunkenness and strife." She takes them because she cannot as the oldest child bear, to see her youngers hurt and struggling, and not help to ease their care.

Do you see her?

Oh! Now do you see me?! Now do you see the pain? Now do you see the poverty? But do you see the joy! I have hope because of you. I have hope because of Jesus!

Do you see me?

I have hope because this school promises me a better life. I have hope because you love me and taught me of Jesus Christ. Will you see the others? Will you give to them? Do you see the poor? Honduras, Kansas City, China and Kentucky; Tennessee and Pakistan, Lebanon and Mali. The poor are all around you.

Do you see them?

Go, and see the poor. They live right next to you. Go and give them hope, because Christ brought hope to you. You need not travel far. If you cannot travel, pray. God will send them where you stay. But obey and serve you must, just as His Word doth say. Do you see them now?

Go you now and see them.

What good is my compassion if it does not move me to act compassionately? Any rebukes and charges and emotional stimulants are to myself as much as you. I am neglectful and willfully ignorant. I do not see them. Lord, help me to see them! I love you Lord. Help me to love you. Help me to love them.

Storytime with Lucky – Alexis Stamatis

~~~~~~

My life is but a weaving,
Between my God and me,
I do not choose the colors,
He worketh steadily,
Oftimes He weaveth sorrow,
And I in foolish pride,
Forget He sees the upper,
And I the underside,
Not till the loom is silent,
And shuttles cease to fly,
Will God unroll the canvas,
And explain the reason why,
The dark treads are as needful,
In the skillful weaver's hand,
As the threads of gold and silver,
In the pattern He has planned.

<div align="right">Anonymous</div>

This Love Story is Better than Any you will find on the Hallmark Channel.

The Bible is a book of love stories: the love of Jacob for Rachel, of Boaz for Ruth, and of Joseph for Mary. But the greatest story is not one of these; rather, it is the story of God's love for ordinary people!

1. It is the story of an unreasonable love. "For God so loved the world . . ."

Unreasonable because God's love is not requested, respected and is seldom reflected. When things go wrong in the world like war, terrorism, homelessness, disease, drug addiction, or political campaigns, people tend to blame God.

The world's response to trouble is to seek diplomatic, judicial, economic, and social solutions. God's love is not respected (valued) because it is viewed as old-fashioned, rigid, and restrictive. God's love is seldom reflected in a world that worships at the altars of success, popularity, and power. In the midst of all of that, God's love breaks through, and He freely loves the world, with what is an irrational and unreasonable love!

2. It is the story of a unreserved love. ". . . that He gave His only Son . . ."

William Gladstone, in announcing the death of Princess Alice in the House of Commons, told a touching story. The little daughter of the Princess was seriously ill with diphtheria. The doctors told the princess not to kiss her little daughter and endanger her life by breathing the child's breath. Once when the child was struggling to breathe, the mother, forgetting herself entirely, took the little one into her arms to keep her from choking to death. Rasping and struggling for her life, the child said, "Momma, kiss me!" Without thinking of herself, the mother tenderly kissed her daughter. She got diphtheria, and some days thereafter she went to be forever with the Lord. - Max Lucado

Real love forgets self. Real love knows no danger. Real love doesn't count the cost. The Bible says, "Many waters cannot quench love, neither can the floods drown it -"Songs 8:7-9. Unreserved is God's gift given freely. Without hesitation, no debates, committees, conferences, or deliberations, what He gave was the only one—unique, incomparable, unmatched, and without equal – His Son! What a unreserved love!

3.   It is the story of an unrestricted love. ". . . that whoever believes in Him . . ."

A certain medieval monk announced he would be preaching next Sunday evening on "The Love of God." As the shadows fell and the light ceased to come in through the cathedral windows, the congregation gathered. In the darkness of the altar, the monk lit a candle and carried it to the crucifix. First of all, he illumined the crown of thorns, next, the two wounded hands, then the marks of the spear wound. In the hush that fell, he blew out the candle and left the chancel. There was nothing else to say. How beautiful is the power of the cross? The cross proclaims loudly that Christ's work on our behalf is a story of unrestricted love in that there are no qualifications to measure up to, achievements to master, or requirements to maintain. The gift of salvation is universal and offered as a free gift to the world.

4. It is the story of an unrestrained love. ". . . should not perish but have everlasting life."

Unrestrained in that God's love for you has no limits (there is nothing it cannot do), knows no bounds (there is no place where it is hindered or ineffective), and it will never end. As the writer of Hebrews describes it, "Your way of life should be free from the love of money, and you should be content with what you have. After all, he has said, I will never leave you or abandon you." Hebrews 13:5. What an unrestrained love!

5. Sadly, it is also a story of an unrealized love.

There are many who have yet to respond or even hear of God's love. "For God did not send His Son into the world to condemn the world, but that the world through Him might be saved. He who believes in Him is not condemned; but he who does not believe is condemned already because he has not believed in the name of the only begotten Son of God" (vv. 17, 18).

At a comparative religions conference, the wise and the scholars were in a spirited debate about what is unique about Christianity. One person suggested that what set Christianity apart from other religions was the concept of incarnation, the idea that God took human form in Jesus. But someone else quickly said, "Well, actually, other faiths believe that God appears in human form." Another suggestion was offered: what about the resurrection? The belief that death is not the final word. That the tomb was found empty. Another participant slowly shook his head.

Other religions have accounts of people returning from the dead.

Then, as the story is told, C.S. Lewis walked into the room, tweed jacket, pipe, arm full of papers, a little early for his presentation. He sat down and took in the conversation, which had by now evolved into a fierce debate. Finally, during a lull, he spoke saying, "what's all this rumpus about?"

Everyone turned in his direction. Trying to explain themselves they said, "We're debating what's unique about Christianity."

"Oh, that's easy," answered Lewis. "It's grace." The room fell silent. Lewis continued that Christianity uniquely claims God's love comes free of charge, no strings attached. No other religion makes that claim.

After a moment someone commented that Lewis had a point, Buddhists, for example, follow an eight-fold path to enlightenment. It's not a free ride. Hindus believe in karma, that your actions continually affect the way the world will treat you; that there is nothing that comes to you not set in motion by your actions.

Someone else observed the Jewish code of the law implies God has requirements. But the beauty of Christianity is that God's grace is completely and totally free. We didn't earn it, we don't deserve it. It was not given to us because we were better than others because we gave more than someone else, we worked harder than another, were more talented, better looking, or more fit.

None of that matters to God. – "What's So Amazing About Grace" - Philip Yancey Hear the text again from the Message Bible:

"This is how much God loved the world: He gave his Son, his one, and only Son. And this is why: so that no one need be destroyed; by believing in him, anyone can have a whole and lasting life. God didn't go to all the trouble of sending his Son merely to point an accusing finger, telling the world how bad it was. He came to help, to put the world right again. Anyone who trusts in him is acquitted; anyone who refuses to trust him has long since been under the death sentence without knowing it. And why? Because of that person's failure to believe in the one-of-a-kind Son of God when introduced to him."

So, our mission is clear, those who know God's love have the privilege to take it to those who have yet to hear, so that they may not only understand the most significant Love Story ever told but receive the full benefits of that love first hand through a life of eternity with God who made your salvation possible.

By Rev. Byrene K. Haney - Blog: http://revheadpin.org

~~~~~~

God's love is meteoric, his loyalty astronomic, His purpose titanic, his verdicts oceanic. Yet in his largeness nothing gets lost; Not a man, not a mouse, slips through the cracks. Anonymous

When you are going through difficulty and wonder where GOD is, remember that the teacher is always quiet during the test. Anonymous

A Medical Sharing Love Story:

It was five years ago that I was told I had a large goiter and needed thyroid surgery. At that time my husband and I were a part of a health care sharing group. We had been told and had learned that this organization would through the help of its members cover the entire cost of medical bills typically associated with this type of surgery.

It was entirely amazing to me that 1. I survived the surgery and 2. Six months after surgery our medical bills had been paid in full through this health care sharing organization. I knew, in the depths of my heart that this was not only as a result of humans reaching out to us but also was God utterly lavishing His great love on not only me, but also on my husband.

If our bills had not been paid in their entirety, I don't think to this day we would be free from medical bills associated with the surgery. The cost was insurmountable to me. It was almost unbelievable. I thought if not for God's grace, we would have been buried in medical bills and would never have seen the light of day again.

This manifestation of God's love to me through people of faith promoted healing and helped me feel more hopeful when going through the initial recovery from surgery. At the time, due to health concerns connected with losing my thyroid, I knew I would not be able to find employment outside the home maybe indefinitely. I was literally at the Lord's mercy, but I never felt hopeless.

Maybe that was due in part to people's prayers and the love family members and friends showed me at the time. God met our immense financial need and knew how to intervene in a way I will never forget.

Our family had experienced severe financial trials prior to this surgery where God had intervened but this time, after surgery, I wasn't so sure we'd weather the storm. I even had doubts about my marriage weathering the storm. It was because of God's wonderful love we navigated through the storm (rejoicing together when we paid the last of the bills off) and since then God has blessed us by adding five new grandchildren to our family.

Since surgery He has continued to show His great love and mercy towards me and in many other instances used other Christians to share His love time and time again.

You can hear that God loves you over and over but until you are really at a point of despair like I was after surgery and in the middle of what could have been a potential financial crisis, you'll never really know HOW MUCH God really loves you. He has shown His love to me in so many other countless ways through many people but this instance, after surgery, is one of the most profound ways, in recent years, that I have ever felt His love poured out on me. **A wife, mother, grandmother and grateful child of the King!**

~~~~~~

God loves each of us as if there were only one of us.
Augustine

By the cross we know the gravity of sin and the greatness of God's love toward us. John Chrysostom

Nothing can separate you from God's love absolutely nothing. God is enough for time, God is enough for eternity. God is enough! Hannah Whitall Smith

A More Excellent Way

We may speak the language of organizational structure and mission, but if we do not have love in our hearts for those who are intended to benefit from our efforts, they will have no more effect than a noisy gong or a clanging cymbal whose influence fades away with its clamor.

We may speak about Servant Leadership and clear lines of authority, we may have compelling strategies for organizational effectiveness and renewal, but if we have not love for people, it is all in vain.

We may distribute our resources with the utmost efficiency and give our lives to save the world, but if love is not our motive, the world will be none the better for our effort.

With love we will be very patient and understanding as we interact with other cultures.

With love we will not feel boastfully righteous as though we have all the solutions to the world's needs.

With love we will never assert our superiority, never selfishly seek praise for sharing with others that with which we have been so abundantly blessed.

With love we will never inflate our ego at the expense of those we have come to serve.

With love we will always be slow to expose the failures and shortcomings of others.

With love we will not be resentful when our service is taken for granted.

Love never gives up. As for theories and strategies, they will be superseded; as for organizations, they will cease. For our planning and our institutions are incomplete, but when our actions are guided by love and justice, they will hit the mark.

We are limited in our understanding; we see in a mirror dimly. We are baffled by problems, and lasting solutions elude us. But we are learning bit by bit and we long for the day when love will rule the world.

Thus, faith that God has a plan for the world, hope that all can realize their human potential, and love that knows no boundaries-these three endure-but the greatest is love. Make love the goal. -Edgar Stoesz, *Doing Good Better (out of print edition)*

~~~~~~

Saving us is the greatest and most concrete demonstration of God's love, the definitive display of His grace throughout time and eternity. David Jeremiah

When the time comes for you to die, you need not be afraid, because death cannot separate you from God's love. Charles Surgeon

The sin underneath all our sins is to trust the lie of the serpent that we cannot trust the love and grace of Christ and must take matters into our own hands. Martin Luther

The Christian does not think God will love us because we are good, but that God will make us good because He loves us. C. S. Lewis

To ask that God's love should be content with us as we are is to ask that God should cease to be God. C.S. Lewis

But the man who is not afraid to admit everything that he sees to be wrong with himself, and yet recognizes that he may be the object of God's love precisely because of his shortcomings, can begin to be sincere. His sincerity is based on confidence, not in his own illusions about himself, but in the endless, unfailing mercy of God. Thomas Merton

One of the greatest evidences of God's love to those that love him is to send them afflictions, with grace to bear them. John Wesley

Give me ... a compassionate heart, quickly moved to grieve for the woes of others and to active pity for them, even as our Lord Jesus Christ beheld our poverty and hasted to help us. Give me grace ever to alleviate the crosses and difficulties of those around me, and never to add to them; teach me to be a consoler in sorrow, to take thought for the stranger, the widow, and the orphan; let my charity show itself not in words only but in deed and truth.

Johann Arndt (1555-1621), German Lutheran theologian who deeply influenced the Pietists

Your accumulated offences do not surpass the multitude of God's mercies: your wounds do not surpass the great Physician's skill."
Cyril of Jerusalem (c.315-386)

Keep on walking in love and don't ever, ever give up for you will reap a reward if you don't quit! Thanks for reading my thoughts and you received anything of value from this little book, please pass it on to someone else! In HIS love - Jeff

About the Author

Dr. Jeff Klick has been in fulltime ministry since 1981. He currently serves as the senior pastor at Hope Family Fellowship in Kansas City, Kansas, a church he planted in 1993. Dr. Klick married his high school sweetheart, Leslie, in May of 1975. They have three adult children and thirteen grandchildren. Dr. Klick loves to learn and has earned a professional designation, Certified Financial Planner, earned a Master's degree in Pastoral Ministry from Liberty Theological Seminary, a Doctorate in Biblical Studies from Master's International School of Divinity, and a Ph.D. in Pastoral Ministry from Trinity Theological Seminary. In addition to serving as senior pastor at Hope Family Fellowship, Dr. Klick is a consultant with The Institute for Church Management and also serves on the Board of Directors for The Council for Gospel Legacy Churches.

www.jeffklick.com

Jeff's Books (available at Amazon.com in print and Kindle)

- *For Our Consideration* – 60 Devotionals and eight in-depth studies to help you and your family grow.
- *Pastoral Helmsmanship* – A team effort from a Seminary Professor, an expert in management, and a pastor to explain in plain English how to navigate church administration.
- *Confessions of a Church Felon* – Our second book to assist pastors and churches in their understanding of and battle against fraud.
- *Courage to Flee, Second Edition* - How to achieve and keep moral freedom.
- *Gospel Legacy: A Church and Family Model* - God's plan for the family explained from a Biblical perspective.
- *The Master's Handiwork* - God is not finished with any of us yet and He never fails, so don't give up or in.
- *Reaching the Next Generation for Christ: The Biblical Role of the Family and Church* - Detailed research on faith impartation to the next generation.
- *The Discipling Church: Our Great Commission* - An in-depth study and training guide on the Great Commission.
- *A Glimpse Behind the Calling: The Life of a Pastor* Written with J. Mark Fox to help both pastors and those who love them.

Made in the USA
Columbia, SC
18 July 2018